SCOTTISH CERTIFICATE OF EDUCA

# Higher HISTORY

The Scottish Certificate of Education Examination Papers
are reprinted by special permission of
THE SCOTTISH QUALIFICATIONS AUTHORITY

ISBN 0 7169 9314 7


*The publishers have wherever possible acknowledged the source of copyright material. They regret any inadvertent omission and will be pleased to make the necessary acknowledgement in future printings.*

**ROBERT GIBSON · Publisher**
17 Fitzroy Place, Glasgow, G3 7SF.

SCOTTISH
CERTIFICATE OF
EDUCATION

# HISTORY
# HIGHER GRADE

## INSTRUCTIONS TO CANDIDATES

### Paper I — Time: 2 hours

Answer questions on ONE Option only.

Take particular care to show clearly the Option chosen. On the front of the answer book, in the top left-hand corner, write A or B or C.

Within the Option chosen, answer THREE questions from at least two sections. One of the sections must be Section (a).

All questions are assigned 25 marks.

Marks may be deducted for bad spelling and bad punctuation, and for writing that is difficult to read.

(Remember that you will have to choose in Paper II a Special Topic from the Option on which you answer questions in Paper I.)

### Paper II — Time: 2 hours

Answer questions on only ONE Special Topic which should be from the Option on which you answered questions in Paper I.

Take particular care to show clearly the Special Topic chosen. On the front of the answer book, in the top left-hand corner, write the number of the Special Topic.

Candidates are expected to use background knowledge appropriately in answering source-based questions.

Marks may be deducted for bad spelling and bad punctuation, and for writing that is difficult to read.

Some sources have been adapted or translated.

SCOTTISH CERTIFICATE OF EDUCATION 1997

WEDNESDAY, 14 MAY
9.30 AM – 11.30 AM

# HISTORY
# HIGHER GRADE
## Paper I

## OPTION A: MEDIEVAL HISTORY

**Answer THREE questions selected from at least two Sections, one of which must be Section (a).**

### Section (a): Medieval Society

1. "In twelfth-century Scotland monks lived comfortable lives which were of no value to society." Discuss.
2. How effectively did the feudal system operate in twelfth-century Scotland and England?
3. Why were towns important in medieval society?
4. Was Henry I's main achievement the maintenance of law and order?
5. Do you agree that Becket was almost entirely to blame for his own death?

### Section (b): Nation and King

6. How far was Magna Carta the result of King John's mishandling of the barons?
7. Was it Louis IX's religious character rather than his ability as a monarch which made him so successful?
8. How important was the contribution of Robert Bruce to Scottish victory in the Wars of Independence?
9. Why did the idea of the Community of the Realm emerge among the barons in England and Scotland but not in France?

### Section (c): Crisis of Authority

10. To what extent can the French victory in the Hundred Years War be attributed to Joan of Arc?
11. Why did serfdom decline in the fourteenth century?
12. How important were national interests in causing the difficulties faced by the Church and Papacy between 1300 and 1450?
13. "The main characteristics of medieval society were all in decay by 1450." Discuss.

1997

## OPTION B: EARLY MODERN HISTORY

**Answer THREE questions selected from at least two Sections, one of which must be Section (a).**

### Section (a): Scotland and England in the Century of Revolutions (1603–1702)

1. Compare the importance of religious and financial issues as threats to royal authority under James VI and I.

2. Would Civil War have broken out in England without the Covenanter movement in Scotland?

3. Why was the monarchy restored in 1660?

4. Did the Revolution of 1688–1689 make important changes to the rights of individuals?

5. How far did the powers of the monarchy in Britain change between 1603 and 1702?

### Section (b): Royal Authority in 17th and 18th Century Europe

6. How real in practice was the growth of royal power in France during Louis XIV's reign?

7. Do you agree that Louis XIV failed to address the religious issue in France effectively?

8. "The description 'Enlightened Absolutism' is a contradiction in terms." How well does the reign of Joseph II illustrate this view?

9. "Here lies a prince whose intentions were pure, but who had the misfortune to see all his plans collapse." To what extent do you accept Joseph II's judgement on himself?

### Section (c): The French Revolution: The Emergence of the Citizen State

10. What was the most serious weakness of the Ancien Régime?

11. Was the nobility the greatest threat to the continuing rule of Louis XVI between 1788 and 1790?

12. Why did the French Revolution become increasingly violent between 1789 and 1794?

13. Which form of government ruled France most effectively between 1793 and 1799?

1997

## OPTION C: LATER MODERN HISTORY

**Answer THREE questions selected from at least two Sections, one of which must be Section (a).**

### Section (a): Britain 1850s–1979

**1.** To what extent did the widening of the franchise change British politics between 1850 and 1928?

**2.** How important a part did events during the First World War play in the decision to grant votes to women?

**3.** "All of the movements failed, swept aside by forces beyond their control." How accurate is this assessment of peace movements in the twentieth century?

**4.** How successful were the welfare reforms of the Labour Government of 1945–1951 in improving social conditions in Britain?

**5.** "Support for Scottish nationalism has been primarily a response to economic hardship." How far would you agree with reference to the period 1930–1979?

### Section (b): The Growth of Nationalism

**6.** How important was the romantic movement in the growth of nationalism in **either** Germany **or** Italy between 1815 and 1848?

**7. Either**

(*a*) "Bismarck's contribution to German unification has been greatly exaggerated." Do you agree?

**Or**

(*b*) To what extent was the unification of Italy made possible by foreign intervention?

**8.** How successful was **either** Germany **or** Italy in dealing with internal political problems between 1871 and 1914?

**9.** "The part played by the leader was decisive in the rise to power of Fascist parties." Discuss this judgement with reference to Germany between 1919 and 1933 **or** Italy between 1918 and 1923.

Hitler

## Section (c): The Large Scale State

### Answer on the USA <u>OR</u> Russia <u>OR</u> China

*The USA*

**10.** Assess the impact of the Wall Street Crash on the American economy in the early 1930s.

**11.** How far was the unequal status of black Americans in the 1920s and 1930s due to the activities of organisations like the Ku Klux Klan?

**12.** To what extent was the growth in the powers of the federal government from the 1930s a result of the need to solve economic and social problems?

**13.** How great an effect did the emergence of black radical movements have on the civil rights movement in the 1960s?

**OR**

*Russia*

**14.** Why was it difficult for opposition movements to make an effective challenge to the Tsarist state in the period before 1905?

**15.** To what extent was the revolution of 1905 caused by government policies?

**16.** How significant were economic problems in causing the outbreak of revolution in Russia in February 1917?

**17.** Assess Lenin's contribution to the success of the Bolshevik revolution of October 1917.

**OR**

*China*

**18.** "A key stage in the development of national identity in modern China." Discuss this view of the May the Fourth movement of 1919.

**19.** How influential were the teachings of Sun Zhongsan (Sun Yat-sen) in the growth and development of the Chinese Communist Party under Mao Zedong (Mao Tse-tung)?

**20.** Did the Great Leap Forward help or hinder China's economic development?

**21.** How accurate is it to describe China as a superpower from the 1960s onwards?

[*END OF QUESTION PAPER*]

SCOTTISH CERTIFICATE OF EDUCATION 1997

WEDNESDAY, 14 MAY
1.00 PM – 3.00 PM

# HISTORY
## HIGHER GRADE
### Paper II
### Sources

| *Option* | | *Special Topic* |
|---|---|---|
| **A Medieval History** | 1 | Norman Conquest and Expansion 1050–1153 |
| | 2 | The Crusades 1096–1204 |
| | 3 | Trade and Towns |
| **B Early Modern History** | 4 | Scotland 1689–1715 |
| | 5 | The Atlantic Slave Trade |
| | 6 | The American Revolution |
| | 7 | The Enlightenment in Scotland |
| **C Later Modern History** | 8 | Patterns of Migration: Scotland 1830s–1930s |
| | 9 | The Third French Republic 1871–1914 |
| | 10 | African Societies and European Imperialism 1880–1914 |
| | 11 | Appeasement and the Road to War, to 1939 |
| | 12 | The Origins and Development of the Cold War 1945–1985 |
| | 13 | Ireland 1900–1985: a Divided Identity |

## SPECIAL TOPIC 1: NORMAN CONQUEST AND EXPANSION 1050–1153

**Study the sources below and then answer the questions in the accompanying question paper.**

**Source A:** Duke William's message to Harold before the Battle of Hastings, from *The Deeds of William, Duke of the Normans and King of the English,* written *c.*1071 by William of Poitiers.

Archbishop Stigand and Earl Godwin, Earl Leofric and Earl Siward, all confirmed by oath and pledge of hands that after Edward's death they would receive me as lord, nor during his lifetime would they seek in any way whatever to prevent my succession to this country . . . Finally, Edward sent Harold himself to Normandy, that he might there swear in my presence what his father and the other aforesaid magnates had sworn in my absence. On his way to me he fell into the peril of captivity, from which I delivered him by the exercise of both prudence and force. He did homage to me and gave me pledge of hand concerning the English kingdom.

**Source B:** Map of the invasions of 1066.

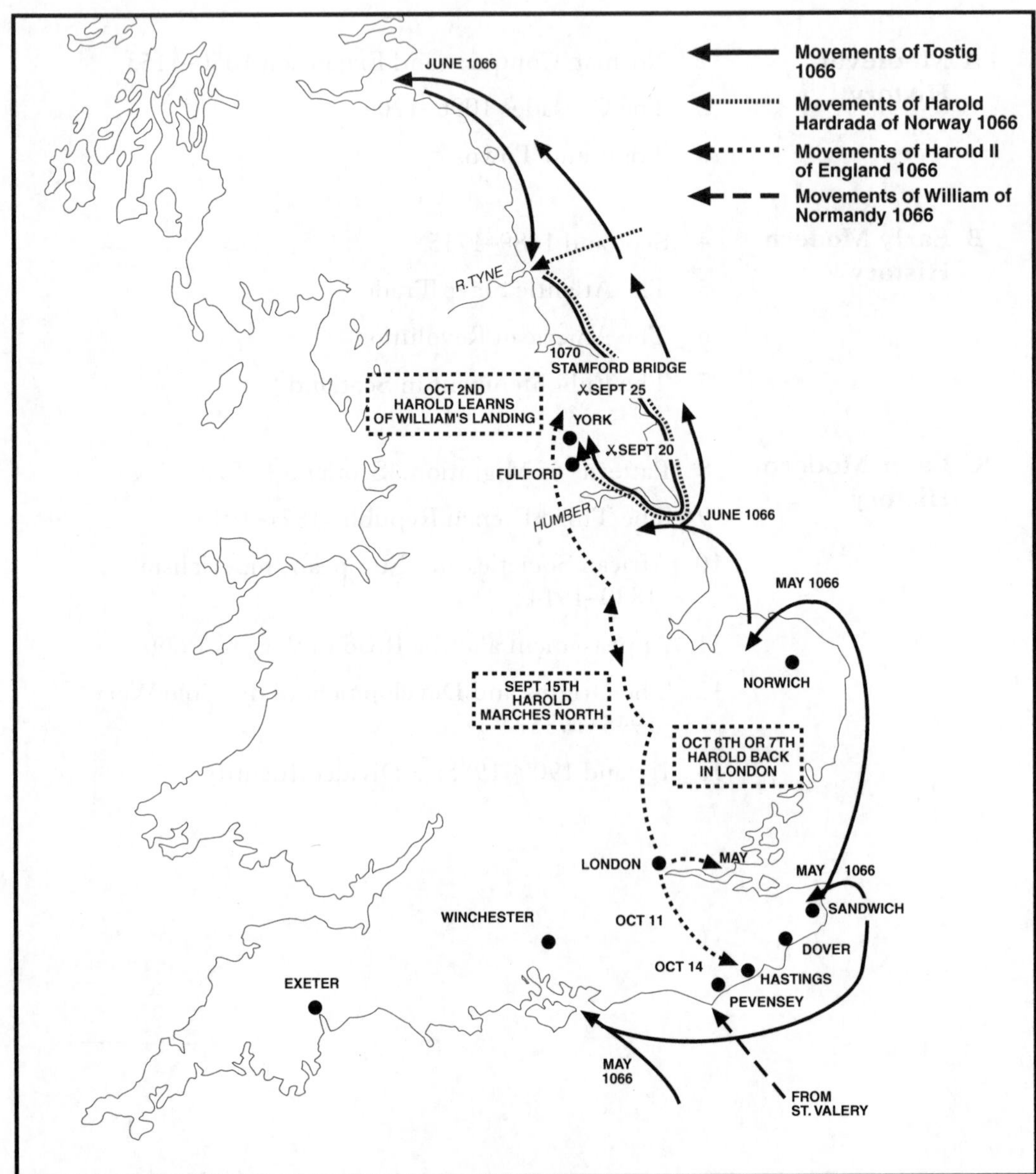

**Source C:** from R.A. Brown, *The Normans and the Norman Conquest* (1985).

Also contributing to a new degree of social cohesion, political unity and royal power was the introduction of feudalism into England, which must be listed high among the most important results of the Norman Conquest. The society of pre-Conquest England was a survival from an older world and cannot in any meaningful way be described as "feudal" in the absence of full feudal commendation[1], in the absence of the fief, and in the absence of native knights and castles. All four fundamental characteristics of contemporary feudal society were rapidly established in England from 1066 onwards, as the Norman duke William, his companions and their knights, brought with them the habits and laws, social relationships and methods of warfare, to which they were accustomed in their home lands, established their lordship over all England, and faced and overcame the problems of its defence. The social revolution involved in the imposition of a new ruling class was accompanied by a revolution in the terms by which the land was held in the upper ranges of society.

[1]commendation—the act of making a person the vassal of a lord by an act of homage

**Source D:** from G.O. Sayles, *The Medieval Foundations of England* (1950).

It is evident that society in England [in 1066] was similar to society in France. There were private relationships between lord and man. There were dependent tenures, like loanland, which were very similar to the fief. There was a nobility with military duties.

It is not reasonable to argue that the Anglo-Saxon social structure was not feudal simply because it did not fully resemble the social structure in Normandy . . . Feudalism is an unsatisfactory word. If, however, what went on in England before 1066 was not feudal the word to describe it will have to be invented.

**Source E:** from the *Book of Ely*, a monastic chronicle written in the mid-twelfth century.

At this time [*c.* 1072] the whole of Scotland with her hordes of warriors sought to rebel against our king William and overthrow him. He, nothing daunted, went against them with a combined force of horse and ships . . . For he had commanded both the abbots and bishops of all England to send their due knight service and he established that from that time forward contingents of knights should be provided by them to the kings of England in perpetual right for their military expeditions, and that no one, however highly placed, should presume to oppose this edict.

**Source F:** an extract for Huntingdon from *Domesday Book*.

In KIMBOLTON Earl Harold had 10 hides taxable. Land for 20 ploughs. Now William of Warenne holds it. He had 5 ploughs in lordship on 5 hides[1];

84 villagers and 36 smallholders with 25 ploughs.

A priest and a church.

Meadow, 70 acres; woodland pasture 1 league long and 1 league wide; 1 mill, 5s.

Value before 1066 £7; now £16 4s.

2 men-at-arms have 1 hide of this land. They have 1 plough and 5 oxen. Value 20s.

In KEYSOE Aellic, 3 virgates[1] of land taxable. Land for 6 oxen.

In jurisdiction.

1 Freeman and 7 smallholders.

Meadow, 4 acres; woodland pastures 50 acres . . .

[1]hide, virgate—measures of areas of land

**Source G:** from M. Lynch, *Scotland, A New History* (1992).

David has been called one of Henry I's "new men", his dependants and colonisers of the north. It was at Henry's insistence that David was granted land and power in southern Scotland by 1113. It was there, as Henry's virtual viceroy in the north, that well before 1124 the characteristic, overlapping layers of Anglo-Norman settlement which would mark his reign as king of Scots were already being planted. A mixed group of Anglo-Norman adventurers settled in Northumbria . . . [There were two sides to David, the Norman feudal side which developed from his role as client and marcher lord of Henry I of England and the Celtic side which came from his being the younger brother of the king of Scots. By 1124 David firmly favoured the feudal side.]

**Source H:** from a charter of David I of Scotland *c.* 1124.

David, King of Scots, to all his barons and men, French and English, greetings.

Know that I give and grant to Robert de Bruce, Annandale and all the land from Nithsdale to the lands of Randolph Meschin. I grant that he hold the land and its castle . . . just as Randolph Meschin held Carlisle in Cumberland . . .

Witnesses. John and Hugh de Morville, . . . William de Somerville, . . . Randolph de Soules . . . at Scone.

[*END OF SOURCES FOR SPECIAL TOPIC 1*]

## SPECIAL TOPIC 2: THE CRUSADES 1096–1204

**Study the sources below and then answer the questions in the accompanying question paper.**

**Source A:** from E. Hallam, *Chronicles of the Crusades* (1989).

The Peace of God had first been proclaimed in France in the last quarter of the 10th century, and was an attempt to protect non-combatants (women, children, the poor, and above all clerics) from the violence of the warrior class. The Truce of God was intended to prevent fighting on Sundays and the great feast days of the Church . . . Urban II proclaimed it among the Normans of southern Italy in 1089, and six years later, at the Council of Clermont. At the same time, he called for the First Crusade, preaching that the knightly class should direct its warlike energies against the infidel, and exercise its tendency to violence in a higher cause than warfare against fellow Christians.

**Source B:** from H.E. Mayer, *The Crusades* (1988).

These [poor] "crusaders" were either badly or not at all armed; above all they lacked the money that was needed for so long a journey . . . Here we can see the immense power which came from Urban II's combination of pilgrimage, war against the heathen, and a spiritual reward. The idea gripped men of all classes; it could not be restricted to the knights . . .

Inflamed by irresponsible preachers and attracted by the wealth of the important Jewish communities of the Rhineland, [the poor crusaders] had indulged themselves in pogroms on a scale hitherto unprecedented in the Middle Ages . . . Frequently the argument that the Jews, as the enemies of Christ, deserved to be punished was merely a feeble attempt to conceal the real motive: greed. It can be assumed that for many crusaders the loot taken from the Jews provided their only means of financing such a journey.

**Source C:** from J. Riley-Smith, *The Crusades* (1990).

It is significant that the first appeal for crusaders was expressed in intimate, even domestic, terms. Men were called upon to go . . . to the aid of their "father" and "lord", Jesus Christ, who was humiliated and disregarded and had lost his inheritance. That was a summons to a vendetta.

The potency of the idea of the vendetta was clearly demonstrated in the opening act of the crusade, the "first holocaust" of European Jews. These pogroms were attributed by some contemporaries to avarice. But the Hebrew accounts ascribed greed more to the local bishops than to the crusaders, who seem to have been more interested in forcing conversions. There is overwhelming evidence that uppermost in the crusaders' minds was a desire for vengeance. They found it impossible to distinguish between Muslims and Jews and if they were being called upon to avenge the injury to Christ's "honour" of the loss of his inheritance to the Muslims, why, they asked, should they not also avenge the injury to his person of the Crucifixion—[carried out by the Jews]?

**Source D:** extracts about the crusaders at Constantinople, from the *Alexiad of Anna Comnena,* written *c.* 1140.

The Emperor, who understood fully Bohemond's wicked intention and perverse mind, skilfully managed to remove whatever might further his ambitious designs. Wherefore, Bohemond, seeking a home for himself in the East and using great scheming, did not obtain it . . . [The emperor] sometimes warned [Raymond of Toulouse] to keep close watch against the malice of Bohemond so as to check him immediately if he should try to break his agreement, and to strive in every way to destroy his schemes. Raymond replied: "Since Bohemond has inherited perjury and deceit, it would be very surprising if he should be faithful to those promises which he has made under oath."

**Source E:** the defeat of the Turkish relief force at Antioch in February 1098, from the *Deeds of the Franks* written *c.* 1100.

The wise man, Bohemond, spoke to the others, "Most invincible knights, array yourselves for battle, each one for himself". They answered, "Great and magnificent man! Brave and victorious man! Decider of battles, and judge of disputes! Make arrangements for us and yourself." Thereupon, Bohemond commanded that each one of the princes should himself form his line in order. They did so, and six lines were formed. Five of them went out together to attack the enemy. Bohemond, accordingly, marched a short distance in the rear with his line . . . As the other lines saw that the standard of Bohemond was so gloriously borne before them, they went back to the battle again, and with one accord our men attacked the Turks, who, all amazed, took to flight.

**Source F:** events of January 1099, from the *History of the Franks who captured Jerusalem*, by Raymond d'Aguilers, written *c.* 1101.

The tears of the poor prevailed, and Raymond set the departure date on the fifteenth day while the infuriated Bohemond proclaimed throughout the town the date of departure as the fifth or sixth day, and soon thereafter returned to Antioch. At the same time the Count requested Godfrey and the absentees from Ma'arrat to come together in one place and make the necessary preparations for resumption of the journey. The princes met and held a conference at Chastel-Rouge, which is almost half way between Antioch and Ma'arrat, but the meeting came to nothing because the leaders and many who followed their example offered reasons for not continuing the journey. As a result Raymond offered Godfrey and Robert of Normandy ten thousand shillings apiece, six thousand to Robert of Flanders, five thousand to Tancred and proportionately to others.

**Source G:** the arrival of the crusaders at Antioch, from *A History of the Expedition to Jerusalem* by Fulcher of Chartres, written between 1101 and 1128.

Antioch is an extensive city, has a strong wall, and is well situated for defence . . . In the city there is a church worthy to be revered, dedicated to the Apostle Peter . . . Also there is another church, round in form, built in honour of the Blessed Mary, and several others fittingly constructed. These had long been under the Turks, yet God, knowing all things beforehand, saved them intact for us, so that at some time or other He would be magnified by us in them.

It happened on a certain day that the Franks killed seven hundred Turks; and the Turks, who set ambushes for the Franks, were overcome by the Franks lying in ambush . . .

Alas! how many Christians—Greeks, Syrians and Armenians—who lived in the city, were killed by the maddened Turks.

**Source H:** events at Jerusalem in June 1199, from H.E. Mayer, *The Crusades* (1988).

Once more a vision came at the critical moment, this time to a priest called Peter Desiderius. He was told that if they held a fast and then a procession round the walls, the city would fall into their hands within nine days—so long as they performed these tasks with sufficient piety.

[*END OF SOURCES FOR SPECIAL TOPIC 2*]

1997

## SPECIAL TOPIC 3: TRADE AND TOWNS

**Study the sources below and then answer the questions in the accompanying question paper.**

**Source A:** map of Stirling in the twelfth and thirteenth centuries.

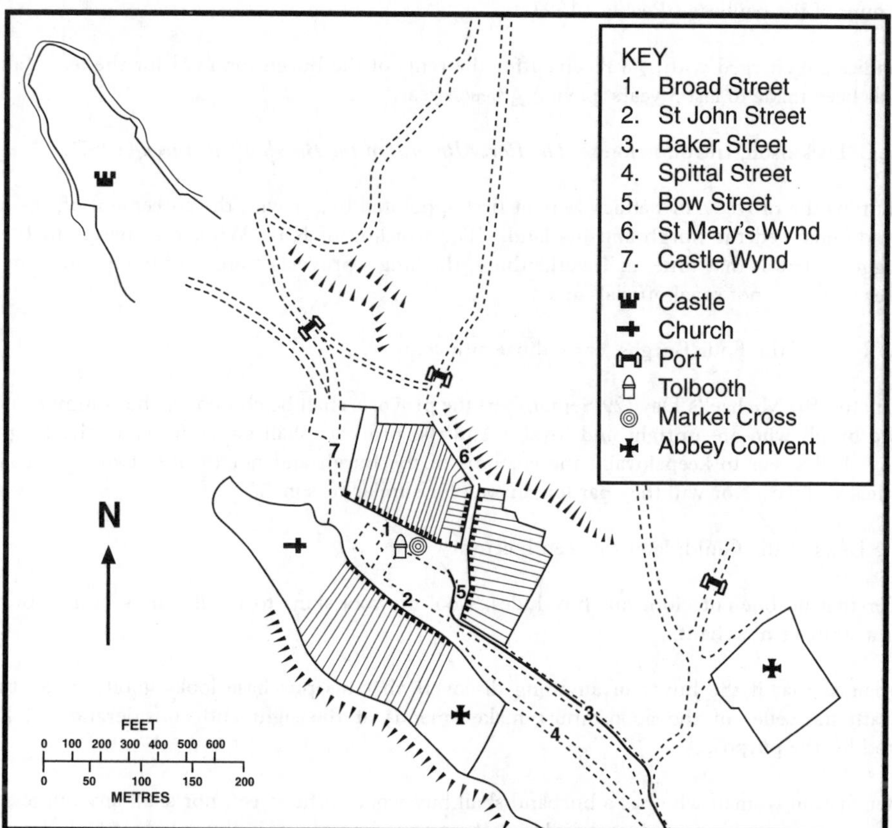


**Source B:** from E. Ewan, *Townlife in Fourteenth-Century Scotland* (1990).

The traveller who had business to transact with the townspeople headed for the centre of the burgh, the market. On market days he would be joined by a steady stream of people bringing produce in from the countryside on horses or wagons or carrying it on their backs or their heads, foreign or local merchants transporting luxuries and other goods from abroad, craftsmen setting up stalls to sell their wares, entertainers, beggars and those who had come to buy. Burghs were generally granted a monopoly on trade in their hinterland, so that certain goods in the region had to be brought to the town for sale. Even on other days of the week, the market was a busy place. It was the centre of burgh life.

**Source C:** from E. Ewan, *Townlife in Fourteenth-Century Scotland* (1990).

There is small evidence of a distinction between merchant and craft guilds until the fifteenth century, about a century later than in England and much later than on the continent. The distinction between craftsman and merchant was only just starting to be made in the fourteenth century. Craftsmen who bought their own materials and sold their own products were as likely to see themselves as merchants as those who bought and sold the work of others. In smaller burghs, especially, the size of the population would have precluded the formation of several separate guilds. In larger burghs such as Aberdeen, the lack of craft guild bequests to altars in the burgh church before the fifteenth century suggests that the crafts did not formally organise themselves into guilds until then.

**Source D:** extracts from *The Exchequer Rolls.*

(*a*) The account of Maurice Hunter and of Finlay, soutars, provosts of the burgh of Stirling. The account was made at Dumbarton on 25 January 1327 for the rents of the burgh. They are charged with £6 for the rents of the burgh.

(*b*) The account of the baillies of Peebles, 1393.

[The baillies are charged with] £8 received for the rents of the burgh for 1393 for the lease [at feu ferme] which has been made to last 5 years, paying £8 each year.

**Source E:** from W.C. Dickinson, Introduction to *The Early Records of the Burgh of Aberdeen* (1957).

Possibly in all burghs the provosts or baillies were at first appointed by, or with the agreement of, the king; for on his behalf they administered the burgh and his land. The wording of King William's charter to Inverkeithing, however . . . suggests that at that time, in Inverkeithing, the king's provosts were simply chosen from among the body of burgesses and were not royal officials apart.

**Source F:** from the Laws of the Four Burghs, early thirteenth century.

At the first court after St. Michael's Day (29 September) the provosts shall be chosen by the common council of the good men of the burgh who are upright and loyal. And the provosts shall swear fealty to the king and to the burgesses. They shall swear to keep loyally the customs of the burgh and not to put anyone on trial to satisfy personal anger, fear or love. Nor will they pardon anyone for similar reasons.

**Source G:** from the Laws of the Guild, later thirteenth century.

23 We order that no one cut cloth nor buy hides, wool or wool skins to resell unless he is a brother of the guild or a stranger merchant.

29 It is ordained that if the buyer of anything discovers that his purchase looks good on top but is worse underneath the seller of the goods must make amends at the sight and consideration of honest men appointed for the purpose.

34 We order that no woman who has a husband shall buy wool in the street; nor shall any burgess have more than one servant to buy wool and hides. If anyone unreasonably buys wool or hides beyond the appointed market time to the detriment of the burgh community the said wool or hides shall be taken for use of the guild and the man or his servant will be fined 8 shillings.

**Source H:** from M. Lynch, "Towns and Townspeople in Fifteenth-Century Scotland", in J.A.F. Thomson (ed.), *Towns and Townspeople in the Fifteenth Century* (1988).

The trade battleground amongst the Scottish burghs had been in wool in the fifty years after the loss of Berwick, Scotland's premier wool town, in 1334. By the second half of the fifteenth century, the battleground had shifted to the trade in hides and skins.

**Average annual custom paid (in £ Scots) on exported hides, 1445–99**

| | 1445–9 | 1455–9 | 1465–9 | 1475–9 | 1485–9 | 1495–9 |
|---|---|---|---|---|---|---|
| Edinburgh | 91 | 111 | 55 | 180 | 95 | 235 |
| Inverness | 45 | 34 | 13 | 3 | - | 3 |
| Perth | 30 | 13 | 10 | 16 | 8 | 9 |
| Aberdeen | 28 | 28 | 12 | 20 | 14 | 12 |
| Linlithgow | 28 | 20 | 22 | 13 | 5 | 3 |
| Kirkcudbright | - | 17 | 20 | 25 | 4 | 3 |

[*END OF SOURCES FOR SPECIAL TOPIC 3*]

## SPECIAL TOPIC 4: SCOTLAND 1689–1715

**Study the sources below and then answer the questions in the accompanying question paper.**

**Source A:** from R.C. Temple, *The Tragedy of the Worcester* (1930).

The Scots were an energetic commercial nation whenever the political condition of the country admitted general attention to commerce, and their jealousy of England, aroused by the Navigation Act, was immeasurable, but, whenever attempts to rival the English monopoly were made, the English merchants, from their entrenchments behind the Navigation Act and its successors, pursued the Scots interlopers and ruined them. This did not cause the Scots to desist, and the Darien Company was only one of many efforts of this kind. Indeed, the attempts never ceased, even after the disastrous failure of that mighty venture; and in consequence, in the end, there was nothing for it but union with England, or, as an alternative, endless fighting between two close neighbours. The Union of 1707 eventually brought this sort of trouble successfully to a close.

**Source B:** from Andrew Fletcher of Saltoun, *An Account of a Conversation concerning a right regulation of Governments* (1703).

I am of opinion, said I, that by an incorporating union, as they call it, of the two nations, Scotland will become more poor than ever.

Why so?

Because Scotsmen will then spend in England ten times more than they do now; which will soon exhaust the money of the nation. For besides the sums that members of parliament will every winter carry to London, all our countrymen, who have plentiful estates, will constantly reside there.

**Source C:** from James Hodges, *The Rights and Interests of the two British Monarchies* (1703).

The English are to retain their distinct sovereignty, independent state and national privileges and dignity after the same manner as they did before enjoy them, with what addition the accession of Scotland can make. All these benefits are lost to Scotland and taken by England in an incorporating union [which] contradicts the first fundamental rule of union, that an union of both must be founded in the interest of both . . . In a large measure it frustrates the concord, security, good understanding and the mutual satisfaction, service and assistance, which are among the chief effects of a happy union. Instead, it disposes to complaints, grudging, resentment, division, separation, devising and pushing on internal commotions and rebellions, and encouraging assaults from foreign enemies. These are among the principal effects of an unhappy union, which an incorporating is here proved to be.

**Source D:** from Daniel Defoe, *The History of the Union between England and Scotland* (1709).

Whatever loss some may allege Scotland suffers in this Union, in matters of commerce, in removing her parliaments, in lessening the assembly of her nobility and gentry in Edinburgh, in taxes and in carrying away her people, these are things which time may remedy and repay her for with interest. Yet this the most prejudiced man in Scotland must acknowledge they have in exchange, and which, if they know how to value it, is worth all they have paid or can pay for it. I mean Liberty in its due and best extent, religious and civil.

**Source E:** from a letter, Daniel Defoe to Harley, 13 September 1703.

I beg leave to set down how I understand my present business as follows:

1. To inform myself of the measures being taken or parties being formed against the Union and apply myself to oppose them.
2. In conversation and by all reasonable methods to dispose people's minds to the Union.
3. By writing or discourse, to answer any objections, libels or reflections on the Union, the English or the Government, relating to the Union.

**Source F:** from Rosalind Mitchison, *Lordship to Patronage* (1983).

Trade and religion were thus motives mutually in opposition. In practice Union would have to be devised by the politicians, the small group who provided holders of office. For these, trade was more important than religion, but at any moment the permanent enrichment of the family of an individual would take precedence over other motives, for that was what sent men into politics. The course by which the country headed for Union was bound to be erratic. One crucial step was the breakaway from the opposition country party of what came to be called either the "new" party or the "Squadrone Volante", a group of frustrated politicians anxious for office, and led by the marquess of Tweeddale.

**Source G:** from David Daiches, *Scotland and the Union* (1977).

The three parties active in the new session of parliament [1706] were the Court Party, supporters of the Government, consisting now mostly of Whig Ministers; the Country Party, now calling itself the New Party; and the Cavaliers, mostly Jacobites and Episcopalians. The New Party, who refused to go along with the Cavaliers, whom they considered to have deserted them in 1704, and who at the same time remained independent of the Court, were widely known as the "Squadrone Volante". They were essentially an opportunist group, strongly nationalist in feeling and formally standing for the Hanoverian Succession with limitations.

[*END OF SOURCES FOR SPECIAL TOPIC 4*]

1997

## SPECIAL TOPIC 5: THE ATLANTIC SLAVE TRADE

**Study the sources below and then answer the questions in the accompanying question paper.**

**Source A:** from Thomas Phillips, *Journal of a Voyage* (1704).

We have some 30 or 40 Gold Coast negroes, which we buy, and are procured for us there by our factors, to make guardians and overseers of the Whydah[1] negroes and sleep among them to keep them from quarrelling; and in order as well to give us notice, if they can discover any plotting among them, which trust they will discharge with great diligence.

[1]Whydah—a port on the Gulf of Benin

**Source B:** from Thomas Clarkson, *The Abolition of the Slave Trade* (1808). The caption to the illustrations said that Clarkson bought the articles in a shop in Liverpool as examples of the ways in which slaves were treated.

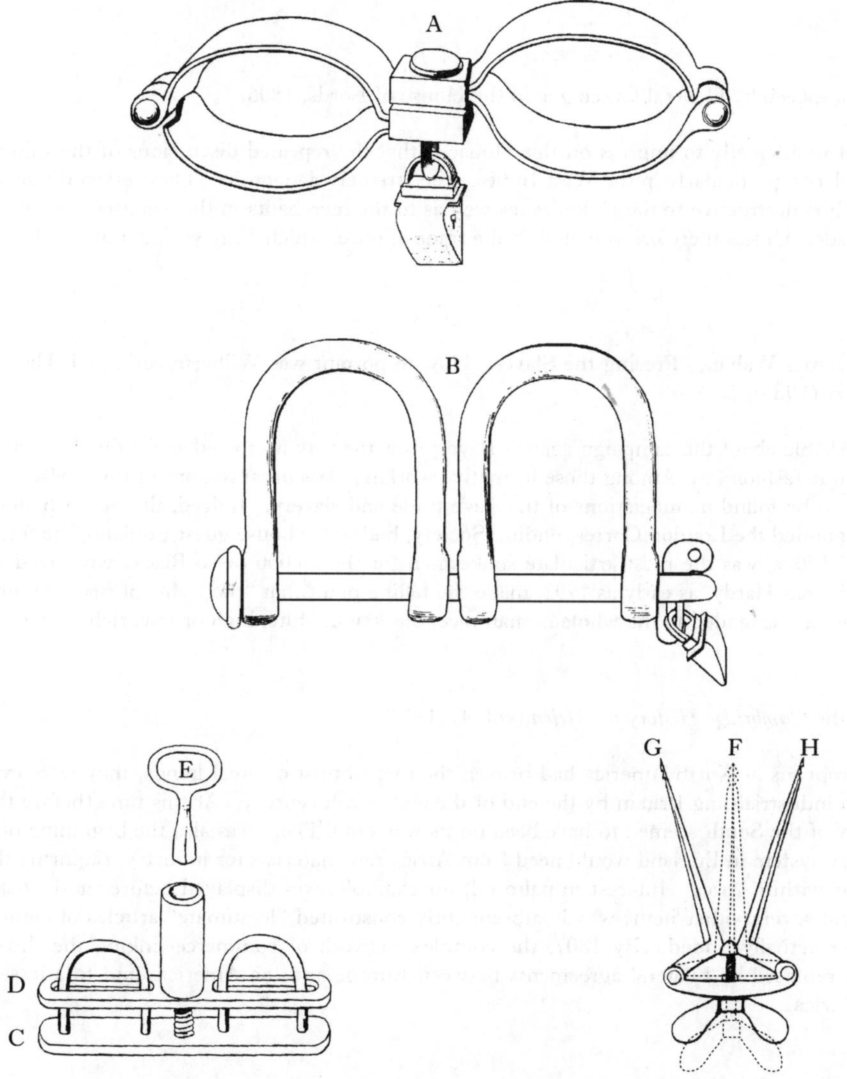


(A) Hand-Cuffs for Slaves (B) Leg Shackles (C–E) Thumb Screws
(F–H) "Speculum Oris" to Open Closed Jaws

**Source C:** from James Walvin, "Freeing the Slaves: How important was Wilberforce?", in J. Hayward (ed.), *Out of Slavery* (1985).

It is when we examine Abolitionist literature, speeches, letters—and artefacts of all kinds—that we begin to edge closer to what the Abolitionists thought and felt about slavery and the slave trade. Above all else, anti-slavery, from first to last, expressed itself most frequently and most stridently in terms of religion.

**Source D:** from a speech by the Bishop of St. Asaph in the House of Lords, 1806.

I am doubtful whether it would be wise, politic, or humane, by any legislative measure, at once, materially, to alter the state of those who are in that unfortunate condition [slavery]. But the question is not concerning the alteration of this condition, but whether you shall abolish the practice by which they are put in that condition. The question now before this House is, whether it is just, humane or politic in us so to place them? I think that question very easily answered. My Lords, any notion of humanity must include a desire of promoting the happiness of every human creature with whom we come in contact, or whose condition, in any degree, depends on us. I know of no justice which is not founded on that golden rule of morals: "to do unto others what we would they should do unto us".

**Source E:** from a speech by General Gascoigne in the House of Lords, 1806.

What I would wish chiefly to impress on this House is that the repeated discussions of the subject in this House, and in other places, particularly in the West Indies, are extremely dangerous. They lessen the security of property, an effect which is destructive to the Colonies, as well as to the merchants in this country who are concerned in the West India trade. Unless therefore you abolish the trade at once, which I say you cannot do, the less you say about it the better.

**Source F:** from James Walvin, "Freeing the Slaves: How important was Wilberforce?", in J. Hayward (ed.), *Out of Slavery* (1985).

What is remarkable about the campaign against slavery was the way it crossed social divides; uniting the nation in an almost unique fashion . . . Among those formative working class organisations of the 1790s—the corresponding societies—are to be found denunciations of the slave trade and slavery. Indeed, the Scottish shoemaker, Thomas Hardy, who founded the London Corresponding Society, had as his house guest Equiano, the former slave who, in the 1780s and 1790s, was the most articulate spokesman for the 20,000 or so Blacks who lived in London at the time. And Thomas Hardy, as early as 1792, made the telling point that "the rights of man are not confined to this small island but are extended to the whole human race, black and white, high or low, rich or poor".

**Source G:** from the *Cambridge History of Africa* (vol. 4) (1975).

Although Europeans in North America had broken the mercantilist colonial bonds, they were even better trading partners of an industrialising Britain by the end of the eighteenth century. At this time (before the cotton era) the slave economy of the South seemed to have been on its way out. There was also the beginning of a new awareness that the factory system in England would need from Africa raw materials for industry, requiring the exploitation of African labour within Africa. Interest in palm oil, for example, was displayed before the British abolition of the slave trade, and several other items which subsequently constituted "legitimate" articles of commerce were being investigated or actually traded. By 1807, the complex network of commerce linking the three continents was already being replaced by bilateral agreements between Europe and the Americas and to a lesser extent between Europe and Africa.

[*END OF SOURCES FOR SPECIAL TOPIC 5*]

1997

## SPECIAL TOPIC 6: THE AMERICAN REVOLUTION

**Study the sources below and then answer the questions in the accompanying question paper.**

**Source A:** from the Declaration of Independence (1776).

When a long train of abuses, pursuing invariably the same Object, demonstrates a design to reduce them under absolute Despotism, it is their right, it is their duty, to throw off such Government, and to provide new Guards for their future security.

Such has been the patient sufferance of these Colonies; and such is now the necessity which constrains them to alter their former System of Government. The history of the present King of Great Britain is a history of repeated injuries and usurpations, all having in direct object the establishment of an absolute Tyranny over these States. To prove this, let Facts be submitted to a candid world.

He has refused his Assent to laws, the most wholesome and necessary for the public good . . .

He has refused to pass other Laws for the accommodation of large districts of people, unless those people would relinquish the right of Representation in the Legislature, a right inestimable to them and formidable to tyrants only.

**Source B:** from the Parliamentary debate on the Coercive Acts, 1774.

*Mr Harris.* I cannot see, sir, any reason for so wide a separation between America and England as other gentlemen think there ought to be. That country, sir, was hatched from this, and I hope we shall always keep it under the shadow of our wings. It has been said, no representation, no taxation. This was the system formerly adopted, but I do not find it authorised in any book of law, nor do I deem it to be a doctrine either reasonable or constitutional. I insist upon it, they are bound to obey both the crown and parliament. The last twelve years of our proceedings have been a scene of inactivity. Let us proceed and improve our method . . .

*Governor Pownal* [former governor of Massachusetts]. Things are now come to action; and I must be free to tell the house that the Americans will resist these measures. They are prepared to do it. I do not mean by arms, but by the conversation of public town meetings. They now send their letters by couriers, instead of the post, from one town to another; and I can say your post office will very soon be deprived of its revenue. With regard to the officers who command the militia of that country, they appoint their own.

**Source C:** an engraving of 1775, believed to be by Philip Dawe.

The Society of Patriotic Ladies at Edenton, North Carolina, signing a document which reads: "We the Ladys of Edenton do hereby Solemnly Engage not to Conform to that Pernicious Custom of Drinking Tea, or that we the aforesaid Ladys will not promote the wear of any Manufacture from England untill such time that all Acts which tend to Enslave this our Native Country shall be Repealed."

**Source D:** from the Olive Branch Petition, 5 July 1775.

Your Majesty's ministers, persevering in their measures, and proceeding to open hostilities for enforcing them, have compelled us to arm in our own defence. They have engaged us in a controversy abhorrent to the affections of your still faithful colonists. When we consider whom we must oppose in this contest, and if it continues, what may be the consequences, our own particular misfortunes are regarded by us only as parts of our distress . . .

Thus called upon to address your Majesty on affairs of such importance to America, and probably to all your dominions, we are earnestly desirous of performing this office with the utmost deference for your Majesty.

**Source E:** from Tom Paine, *Common Sense* (1776).

The Sun never shined on a cause of greater worth. 'Tis not the affair of a City, a County, a Province or a Kingdom; but of a Continent—of at least one eighth part of the habitable globe. 'Tis not the concern of a day, a year or an age; posterity is involved in the contest, and will be more or less affected even to the end of time by the proceedings now.

**Source F:** from C. Bonwick, *The American Revolution* (1991).

For many months Congress was uncertain. A handful of members including the Adams cousins believed separation was essential; John Dickinson and others were convinced that it was not. Many were undecided. For several weeks delegates debated in secret and acted only when compelled by events. On the one hand Congress resolved to promote reconciliation; on the other it resolved that "these colonies be immediately put into a state of defence". In spite of this hesitation, many decisions implicitly pointed towards independence. They advised the New York Provincial Congress to raise militia and prepare to defend the city. They began to organise military supplies, and voted to issue $2,000,000 in paper money . . . In mid-June Congress voted to raise troops in Pennsylvania, Maryland and Virginia for service outside Boston, formed the Continental army and issued a set of military regulations. George Washington of Virginia was elected commander-in-chief on the nomination of John Adams and assumed command of the New England troops at Cambridge, Massachusetts, on 3 July 1775.

**Source G:** from H.H. Peckham, *The Toll of Independence* (1974).

Initially most of the American colonies easily broke away from British rule by expelling their British governors and judges, and ignoring the royally appointed councillors. The burden of restoring and maintaining British authority fell on the mother country, which meant that British arms had to assume the offensive and defeat or destroy the Colonial army and navy.

[*END OF SOURCES FOR SPECIAL TOPIC 6*]

## SPECIAL TOPIC 7: THE ENLIGHTENMENT IN SCOTLAND

**Study the sources below and then answer the questions in the accompanying question paper.**

**Source A:** from W. Gilpin, *Observations made in the year 1776 on the Highlands of Scotland* (1789).

Having thus shown the unfavourable side of the highland character, let us consider it next in a more pleasing light. The whole system of manners indeed which belongs to it, is now wholly changed. You may travel through any part of Scotland, and rarely hear of an atrocious deed. Quarrelling among the chiefs has subsided, and theft and rapine among the inferior orders are at an end.

There are very few instances, in the annals of human nature of a country so suddenly reclaimed. After the battle of Culloden, when the sovereignty of the highland chiefs was abolished by act of parliament, this happy change immediately took place.

**Source B:** from Samuel Johnson, *A Journey to the Western Isles of Scotland* (1775).

The chiefs, stripped of their powers, necessarily turned their thoughts to the improvement of their revenues, and expect more rent, as they have less homage. The tenant is far from perceiving that his condition is made better in the same proportion as that of his landlord is made worse. He does not immediately see why his industry is to be taxed more heavily than before. He refuses to pay the demand, and is ejected. The ground is then let to a stranger, who perhaps brings a larger stock, but who, taking the land at its full price, treats with the Laird upon equal terms, and considers him not as a chief, but as a dealer in land. Thus the estate is perhaps improved, but the clan is broken.

**Source C:** from R.H. Campbell and A.S. Skinner (eds.), *The Origins and Nature of the Scottish Enlightenment* (1982).

Cullen created a non-medical audience for chemical instruction, particularly among those educated members of polite society eager to promote the agricultural and economic improvement of the nation. If agriculture is to be improved by rational investigations, he argued, then chemistry is the science to be employed. Towards the end, he gave special lectures on the principles of agriculture and vegetation, corresponded at length with Lord Kames on the chemistry of fertilisers, and ran his own experimental farm. He believed that "the lands of this country are mostly improvable, and are really improving", and said that while his chemistry course "was intended to teach the elements of a chemistry applicable to arts in general, agriculture claimed a place". Although Cullen's investigations did not lead to any improvements in agricultural practice or productivity, his association of chemistry and agricultural improvement helped improve the status and importance of chemistry and its practitioners.

**Source D:** from Rev. Alexander Carlyle, *Anecdotes and Characters of the Times*, written between 1800 and 1805.

The club they instituted in 1762 called the Militia or the Poker Club, not only included the Literati but many noblemen and gentlemen of fortune and of the liberal professions. They mixed together with all the freedom of convivial meetings once a week during 6 months in the year, which contributed much to strengthen the bond of union among them. Although the great object of those meetings was national, of which they never lost sight, they had also happy effects on private character by forming and polishing the manners which are suitable to civilised society. For they . . . raised the ideas and enlarged the views of the Gentry and created in the several orders a new interest in each other, which had not taken place before in this country.

**Source E:** James Craig's winning design for the New Town of Edinburgh, 1776.

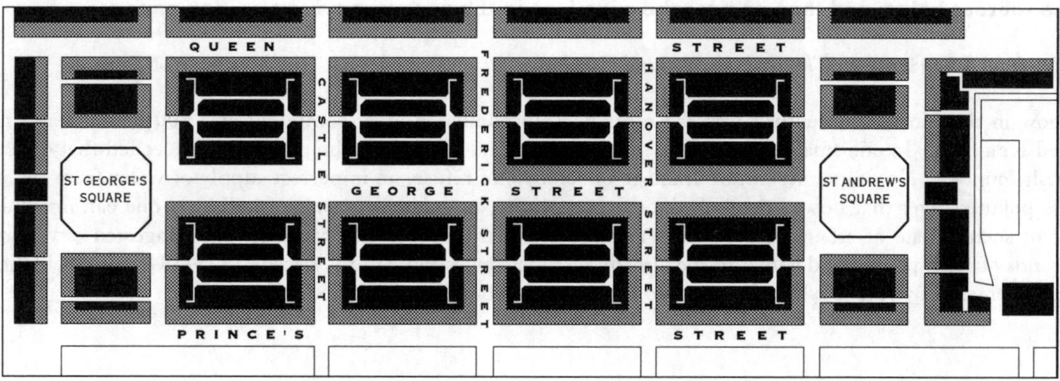


**Source F:** from Rev. Alexander Carlyle, *Anecdotes and Characters of the Times,* written between 1800 and 1805.

It is observable that no country has ever been more tranquil, except the trifling insurrections of 1715 and 1745, than Scotland has been since the Revolution in 1688, a period of 117 years, while at the same time the country has been prosperous, with an increase of agriculture, trade and manufactures, as well as the ornamental arts of life to a degree unexampled in any age and country. How far the steady loyalty to the Crown and attachment to the Constitution, together with the unwearied diligence of the clergy in teaching a rational religion, may have contributed to this prosperity cannot be exactly ascertained. But surely enough appears to entitle them to the high respect of the state and to justice from the country in a decent support to them and to their families.

**Source G:** from Trevor Royle, *Precipitous City* (1980).

Lawyers had always kept open their links with Europe and it was common practice, with the spirit of Scots Law being Roman-Dutch, for the young men to spend a year at a continental university studying law. The connection with Europe was of long standing and although it had been weakened in the years following the Union of the Crowns, it was reborn during the eighteenth century. This was another reason for the rise of the *literati*—a desire to assimilate European thought—and it was common to find writers like the economist Adam Smith urging his fellows to better themselves by studying "foreign" (European) literature and philosophy.

[*END OF SOURCES FOR SPECIAL TOPIC 7*]

1997

## SPECIAL TOPIC 8: PATTERNS OF MIGRATION: SCOTLAND 1830s–1930s

**Study the sources below and then answer the questions in the accompanying question paper.**

**Source A:** from J.E. Handley, *The Irish in Scotland* (1943).

Glasgow in the nineteenth century was the most densely populated area, computed at 5,000 to the acre, in the United Kingdom. In one small rectangular section in the heart of the city, the population exceeded that of several Scottish counties. No proper system of drainage or removal of refuse, an imperfect supply of water from the more or less polluted river that flowed through the city, no privies, no baths or means of bathing—one can imagine the effect of such a state of affairs in the health and morals of the people. It was into this congested city that the thousands of Irish poured and added to the already terrible congestion. In the decade 1831–1841 the population of the city increased by 78,000 while the number of new houses built was only 3,551.

**Source B:** from the *Report on the Sanitary Condition of Edinburgh*, 1854.

The crusts of filth were in some places six inches thick . . . No water supply laid on, no domestic conveniences, no means of removing solid refuse or fluid refuse but by the laborious practice of removal down or up stairs in vessels . . . or by the more speedy and general practice of scattering it on the neighbouring surface . . . No sinks or drain pipes are there, no ventilation, no light, no water supply. All is disgusting, degrading and brutalising beyond description.

**Source C:** from the *Report on the State of the Irish Poor in Great Britain*, 1836.

The poor Irish frequently lie on the floor, on straw or shavings; frequently, however, they have beds. It is the practice for as many to sleep in the same bed as can be crowded into it—frequently three or four beds are in the same apartment, in which males and females sleep next to one another . . . The Irish are, in general, dirtier and less well clothed than the native population.

In consequence of the crowded state of the Irish lodging houses, typhus has prevailed in Glasgow among the Irish more extensively than among the Scotch. During the operations of the fever committees, they have often been obliged to shut up these lodging houses, and fumigate and whitewash them in order to prevent contagion . . . The lowest part of the working population being Irish, we find that in comfort, education and moral feeling, they are inferior to the Scotch. The Irish are more indifferent to education than the Scotch, and education does not prevail so extensively among them.

**Source D:** from *Inquiry into Vice and Destitution in Edinburgh*, 1850.

You may find that this degradation is to a very great extent the result of idleness and drunkenness, and also owing to the neglect of their duty by those who have the means in their power to do good to their fellow creatures.

Especially and emphatically, I blame the clergy who, holding an express commission to seek out the lost and wretched, discharge almost none of these duties . . . In a great many of these wretched places . . . I found that the unhappy inmates knew not even the names of their parish ministers . . . I hope that I am not to be impudently told that this is the blame of these wretched creatures . . . It is ten thousand times more the blame of the ministers of the Gospel . . . It is his business, if any of his parishioners, from wretchedness or wickedness, will not go to him, to go to them and introduce himself to them, not waiting till the request for an introduction come from the other side.

**Source E:** from T.M. Devine, *Clanship to Crofters' War: the Social Transformation of the Highlands* (1994).

A sense of ethnic identity was preserved and strengthened by religion, education, parish social life and the hostility of the host community. Residential patterns in the cities and Irish dominance of specific employments also added to a continuing collective awareness which was maintained into subsequent generations. How far this model can be applied to the Highlanders is much less certain. There is evidence of continued ethnic awareness with the building in several towns of Gaelic chapels, the foundation of Highland Societies and the proliferation of Highland clubs of various sorts. These organisations mainly attracted middle-class migrants for "social" reasons and were ignored by many ordinary Highlanders. The Gaelic churches did have a much more popular appeal but they did not perform the same role played by the Catholic chapels as centres of a distinct identity for the Irish and only a minority of Highland migrants had any formal connection with the Gaelic churches.

**Source F:** from R. Somers, *Letters from the Highlands (after the Great Potato Famine of 1846)* (1848).

Parishes in the Highlands are as large as many English counties, and to each of these the parochial system usually gives but one school. The position of the population has also been changed recently, so that the parochial schools are frequently very difficult of access even to the majority of the parishioners. The fishing villages, for example, are all recent creations, which were not contemplated when the sites of many of the schools were selected. It is usual to find one of these villages, with a population of 300 or 400, without a school within several miles. The number of uneducated children must necessarily be immense. In 1833, the General Assembly's Committee found that, in a district with a population of 151,053, there were no fewer than 55,718 persons, above the age of six years, unable to read in any language. In 1837, it was found by the Glasgow Destitution Committee that, in the same district, with the population increased to 154,763, the number of schools had fallen from 328 to 266, and the number of scholars from 16,891 to 13,586! An inquiry at the present day would probably fail to exhibit any more satisfactory results.

**Source G:** from R.D. Anderson, *Education and Opportunity in Victorian Scotland* (1983).

In the old Scotland, social distances had been relatively short below the gentry level: farmers, artisans, shopkeepers and lesser professional men could make similar demands on education and share a common culture based on their religious life. But with industrialisation and urbanisation . . . strains appeared. The towns contained both a growing mass of semi-skilled and unskilled workers for whom education beyond the basics did not seem a pressing need, and an expanding and multi-layered middle class with new professional and practical needs. This middle class required more formal qualifications in a society which was becoming more complex and more achievement-oriented, but it also valued education for reasons of status.

[*END OF SOURCES FOR SPECIAL TOPIC 8*]

1997

## SPECIAL TOPIC 9: THE THIRD FRENCH REPUBLIC 1871–1914

**Study the sources below and then answer the questions in the accompanying question paper.**

**Source A:** from Jules Ferry, *Revue Pedagogique* (1882).

This is the greatest and most serious of social reforms and the most lasting of political reforms . . . When the whole of French youth has developed, grown up under this free, compulsory, secular education we shall have nothing more to fear from returns to the past, for we shall have the means of defending ourselves . . . The spirit of all these new generations, of these countless young reserves of republican democracy, trained in the school of science and reason, will block retrograde attitudes with the insurmountable obstacle of free minds and liberated consciences.

**Source B:** from a speech by Georges Clemenceau, 1894.

When I read the history of these wretched teachers, alternately scolded by the prefect for their indifference, rewarded by the deputy they have served, and reviled and disgraced by whomsoever they have opposed, it has seemed to me that the unfortunate schoolmaster is truly the most pitiable victim of our glorious Republic . . . In futile efforts the pitiful ambassador of the Republic to the inhabitants of the rural districts consumes his time and his strength. The parents are inaccessible to him; the country squires are his enemies. With the priest there is latent hostility; with the Catholic schools there is open war. The latter have at their disposal greater resources than the teacher. They steal his pupils. They crush him in a hundred ways . . . The government, which should defend him but which often abandons him, is far away. The Church, which persecutes him, is very close at hand . . . Today's deputy defends him; tomorrow's sacrifices him. He is spied upon, hounded, denounced.

**Source C:** from J.P.T. Bury, *France 1814–1940* (1969).

After their experience of the rule of Moral Order between 1873 and 1877 there was hardly a Republican who could not have been firmly convinced that the power of the Church had increased, was increasing and ought to be diminished. Accordingly, when in 1876 Gambetta, echoing a cry already uttered in the 'sixties, thundered "Clericalism—there is the enemy", he knew that he would rally Republicans of every shade. It was therefore both natural and logical that the first big offensive of the Republicans to consolidate their power should be anti-clerical in direction. But it was also a happy coincidence that such a policy was likely to win the approval of such powers as Germany, Italy and Austria, which were at this time concerned with their own struggles of Church and State.

**Source D:** from a toast by Cardinal Lavigerie, 12 November 1890.

Confronted with a past that is still bleeding, and an ever menacing future, we are at this moment in supreme need of union. The union of all good citizens is also the prime hope of the Church and its pastors of every rank in the hierarchy.

Union does not demand that we should renounce the memories of past glories, or the feelings of fidelity and gratitude which honour all men. But when the will of a people has been clearly stated, that the form of government, as Leo XIII recently proclaimed, contains nothing in itself contrary to the principles which alone can give life to Christian civilised nations, when there is no other way of saving one's country from the disaster that threatens it than by adhering unreservedly to that form of government, then the moment has come to declare finally that the testing time is over, and to put an end to our differences. The time has come to sacrifice all that conscience and honour will permit. Each one of us must make sacrifice for the salvation of the country.

**Source E:** from J-M. Mayeur and M. Rebérioux, *The Third Republic from its Origins to the Great War* (1984).

Wishing to apply remedies to the social question and eager to make converts, priests and militants also wanted to reconcile the Church and the Republic, and took up Leo XIII's invitation to rally to the Republic . . . The reasons for the Ralliement were complex . . . The personal role of Leo XIII was considerable. Since his accession in 1878 he had always displayed moderation in his relations with the Republic . . . He had repeatedly let it be understood that French Catholics should accept the country's institutions. After the elections of 1889 he thought it was essential to intervene. He was guided by a number of different aims: he wanted to assert the distinction between the spiritual authority and the temporal authority, to break the links between French Catholics and the monarchy, and to safeguard the Concordat and the state subsidy to religion—which was threatened by the radicals—by enabling the conservatives and the moderate republicans to come to an understanding . . .

These preoccupations struck a chord with some conservative politicians, who thought it pointless to go against public opinion. Acceptance of the régime seemed inevitable.

**Source F:** from a speech by Charles Dupuy at Toulouse, 23 May 1893.

I recognise that unlike their ancestors they have learned something. But they will be the first to agree with me that they have forgotten nothing, not even the way to the royalist committees where doubtless they are planning some parallel action, or even a convergent one. I accept that they will endure the Republic; I am asking whether they would defend it!

**Source G:** from Alfred Cobban, *A History of Modern France vol 3: 1871–1962* (1965).

If survival was a test of political success, the Third Republic had passed it. By 1914 it had long outlasted all previous régimes since 1789. Its economic progress had been slow, but only in comparison with that of the more advanced industrial countries. The status and economic conditions of the peasantry, who constituted the largest section of the French nation, had risen to the point at which it would not have been very exaggerated to describe France as a peasants' republic. What, more than anything else, made this one of the great ages of French history was its achievement in arts, letters and sciences . . .

Literature and politics met and influenced one another in the cafés of the Left Bank, but the spirit of the greater literature, as of the painting and music of the Third Republic, rose above its passing political interests. By its writers and painters and musicians, even if the society of their time failed to recognise their full stature, the Third Republic becomes one of the great ages of French history.

[*END OF SOURCES FOR SPECIAL TOPIC 9*]

## SPECIAL TOPIC 10: AFRICAN SOCIETIES AND EUROPEAN IMPERIALISM 1880–1914

**Study the sources below and then answer the questions in the accompanying question paper.**

**Source A:** from F.D. Lugard, *The Rise of our East African Empire vol. 1* (1893).

The "Scramble for Africa" by the nations of Europe . . . was due to the growing commercial rivalry, which brought home to the civilised nations the vital necessity of securing the only remaining fields for industrial enterprise and expansion. It is well, then, to realise that it is for our *advantage*—and not alone at the dictates of duty—that we have undertaken responsibilities in East Africa. It is in order to foster the growth of the trade of this country, and to find an outlet for our manufactures and our surplus energy, that our farseeing statesmen and our commercial men advocate colonial expansion.

There are some who say we have no *right* in Africa at all, that "it belongs to the natives". I hold that our right is the necessity that is upon us to provide for our ever-growing population—either by opening new fields for emigration, or by providing work and employment which the development of overseas extension entails—and to stimulate trade by finding new markets, since we know what misery trade depression brings at home.

**Source B:** from J. Iliffe, *Africans: The History of a Continent* (1995).

There had been no single European motive for the partition. Africa was not central to European economies: during the 1870s it accounted for little more than 5 per cent of Britain's trade, most of it with Egypt and South Africa. Commercial interests in tropical Africa were vital to annexations on the west coast, but elsewhere merchants such as the Germans in Zanzibar often opposed colonial conquest lest it disrupt existing trade. Successful businessmen left risky colonial investments to less prosperous competitors or to enthusiasts with non-commercial motives. Rhodes's British South Africa Company never paid a dividend during the thirty-three years it administered Rhodesia.

**Source C:** from B. Porter, *The Lion's Share: A Short History of British Imperialism 1850–1983* (1984).

The German coup in east Africa seemed to be as much of a surprise to the government as their exploits in the west . . . Gladstone tried to pretend it did not matter, but it clearly did, because at a stroke it destroyed the basis of British supremacy and security in the area. The Sultan of Zanzibar was no longer the dominant authority on the east African coast, and so he was no use any more as a puppet. Britain's bluff in east Africa had been called.

Neither Bismarck nor Salisbury felt very strongly about east Africa . . . What made Salisbury change his mind, was partly the appearance of financial solidity which Mackinnon was able to give to his company during that year . . . and partly the government's own reassessment of the dangers which threatened Britain's national interests in east Africa. There was considerable disquiet in the Foreign Office about what was happening in Uganda in the Lakes region.

**Source D:** from a Foreign Office memorandum for the Cabinet, prepared by Rosebery, Secretary of State for Foreign Affairs, 16 September 1892.

Uganda has become a question of Imperial policy.

In the first place, there is the question of the Nile. At present we are the only civilised nation that has access to the Nile, and in view of the vital interest of the Nile to Egypt, and the peril to Egypt of any diversion of its stream, it is extremely important that we should remain so. But other nations are anxious to obtain a footing on it . . . France herself is making for the Nile from the west by trying to force down the boundary line with the Congo State, so as to give her a route to the Nile from her possessions in the French Congo. Italy on the east is pushing in the same direction. Germany would probably take advantage of our evacuation to step in. Uganda is no doubt outside her sphere of influence. But if we go, and there is a chaos of blood and destruction after our departure, the Germans, whom the Catholics have already thought of summoning, will have a right, in the name of humanity, to come and occupy this long coveted territory, and to take up the civilising work that we have abandoned as beyond our strength. It may not be possible permanently to preserve the Nile for Great Britain and for Egypt, but if we abandon Uganda, we lose at once and by that fact the control of the Nile.

**Source E:** from Colin Cross, *The Fall of the British Empire* (1968).

Africa lay on the way to India and whether the route were around the Cape or through the Suez Canal it was regarded as essential to prevent hostile European powers establishing bases there . . . British pioneers on the spot could always claim London support by using the argument of communications with India. The most obvious chain of conquest on these lines had been that in East Africa. To protect the Suez Canal it was regarded as essential to control Egypt. To control Egypt it was essential to control the hinterland, Sudan. To control Sudan and the source of the Nile, on which Egypt depended, it was necessary to control Uganda. To control Uganda it was necessary to have a railway running from the East Coast.

**Source F:** from S.R. Karugire, *A Political History of Uganda* (1980).

A Liberal Government was returned to power in 1892 at a time when the question of retaining Uganda (which meant the kingdom of Buganda) was something of a public debate. This tended to confirm the view that the British reluctantly accepted the "burden" of administering Uganda in order to accommodate the pressure of missionaries and their allies in Britain. Much of the propaganda for retaining Uganda was centred on the "precarious" situation of the missionaries "labouring" in Uganda and, of all things, the suppression of the slave trade. The fact that the disorders that were raging in Buganda had been caused by the missionaries was ignored . . .

It was not the safety of the missionaries or an invitation from Mutesa . . . which led the British to come to Uganda. To believe this is to ignore the wider strategies of imperialism which made such factors side issues.

**Source G:** an Arab poem from North Ghana, written in 1900.

A sun of disaster has risen in the West,
Glaring down on people and populated places.
Poetically speaking, I mean the catastrophe of the Christians,
The Christian calamity has come upon us
Like a dust cloud.
At the start of the affair they came
Peacefully,
With soft sweet talk.
"We've come to trade!!" they said.
"To reform the beliefs of the people,
To halt oppression here below, and theft,
To clean up and overthrow corruption",
Not all of us grasped their motives,
So now we've become their inferiors,

They deluded us with little gifts
And fed us tasty foods . . .
But recently they've changed their tune.

[*END OF SOURCES FOR SPECIAL TOPIC 10*]

1997

## SPECIAL TOPIC 11: APPEASEMENT AND THE ROAD TO WAR, TO 1939

**Study the sources below and then answer the questions in the accompanying question paper.**

**Source A:** from the *Broughty Ferry Guide, Carnoustie Gazette and Monifieth Advertiser,* 14 March 1936.

We firmly believe that the great majority of the British people, while admitting that Hitler's action is dangerous, are convinced in their own minds that it is in many ways justifiable. It has at least brought matters to a head and every effort should be made to see that pig-headed French statesmen do not again make a mess of things.

The British people do not wish to fight anyone. But they are getting tired of French methods, which they recognise to have been the cause of all the trouble. The British nation is still anxious for a settlement which will bring an era of peace to Europe. But that will not be achieved unless due attention is paid to Germany's appeal for fairness in preference to the one-sided demands usually made by France. France must be given to understand that Germany is claiming nothing that is out of place; that her demands are considerably more justifiable than many that have been made and are being made by France.

**Source B:** from R.A.C. Parker, *Chamberlain and Appeasement* (1995).

Two facts determined the course of the so-called "Rhineland crisis". One was the French decision to take counteraction only in collaboration with the British; the other the, entirely predictable, British decision to do nothing to damage a renewed attempt to come to terms with Germany. The real crisis lay in Franco-British diplomacy. The French Foreign Minister, Flandin, needed to show that they had been firm with the evasive British and had compelled them to do something serious to resist Germany; the British government needed to show most of its public the reverse, that it did not intend to risk a quarrel with Germany.

**Source C:** from a report to the Cabinet by the Chiefs of Staff, 8 December 1937.

It will be seen that our Naval, Military and Air Forces, in their present stage of development are still far from sufficient to meet our defensive commitments, which now extend from Western Europe through the Mediterranean to the Far East . . . Without overlooking the assistance which we should hope to obtain from France, and possibly other allies, we cannot foresee the time when our defence forces will be strong enough to safeguard our territory, trade and vital interests against Germany, Italy and Japan simultaneously. We cannot, therefore, exaggerate the importance, from the point of view of Imperial defence, of any political or international action that can be taken to reduce the numbers of our potential enemies and to gain the support of potential allies.

**Source D:** from Cabinet minutes, 12 March 1938, reporting comments by Neville Chamberlain on the Anschluss.

The manner in which the German action in Austria had been brought about was most distressing and shocking to the world and was a typical illustration of power politics. This made international appeasement more difficult . . . In spite of all, however, he felt that this thing had to come. Nothing short of an overwhelming display of force would have stopped it . . . At any rate, the question was now out of the way.

**Source E:** from a speech by Lt. Commander Fletcher MP in the House of Commons, 14 March 1938.

This coup in Austria has been along the usual lines . . . We make representations; we are very pained and grieved . . . We send a protest; we are giving the situation continuous attention . . .

Assurance after assurance has been given in this House and by the Government on the subject of Austrian independence. Herr Hitler has shown himself a very shrewd judge of what those assurances were worth. Democracy has been beaten again, and yet we go on expecting small countries which live in the path of Germany's next advance to stick to their belief in democracy . . .

It is the latest, but it will not be the last, of the series of humiliating diplomatic defeats which we have had to endure ever since 1931. One humiliation, one defeat after another . . . Ever since 1931, there has been a steady diminution of our influence and, what is worse, a steady loss of friends.

**Source F:** a cartoon by David Low in the *Evening Standard*, 4 October 1938.

"Our new defence."

**Source G:** from Martin Kitchen, *Europe between the Wars* (1988).

Neville Chamberlain . . . felt that appeasement was an urgent necessity and he followed this policy with a single-minded determination lacking in any of his predecessors. War had to be avoided at all costs because he believed that the money should be spent on social welfare programmes rather than armaments . . . He strongly disliked the Soviet Union, had no faith in the French and believed that the United States was unshakably isolationist. The service chiefs warned him that Britain was in no position to fight Germany, Italy and Japan, thus confirming his own fears which were intensified when Italy joined the Anti-Comintern Pact in September 1937 . . . Chamberlain prided himself on being a practical man and imagined that Hitler and Mussolini were at heart equally practical men with whom it was possible to negotiate in good faith. This belief in himself as a practical man was combined with a strong sense of mission, resulting in a rigidity, an inability to adjust to unpleasant facts and a narrowness of vision which in the end proved disastrous. Hitler was able to exploit these weaknesses to the full to win a series of cheap victories which in turn stimulated his lust for further triumphs.

[*END OF SOURCES FOR SPECIAL TOPIC 11*]

## SPECIAL TOPIC 12: THE ORIGINS AND DEVELOPMENT OF THE COLD WAR 1945–1985

**Study the sources below and then answer the questions in the accompanying question paper.**

**Source A:** from the Sixteen Demands of Budapest's Technological University, posted throughout Budapest, 23 October 1956.

1 We demand the immediate evacuation of all Soviet troops . . .

2 We demand the election by secret ballot of all Party members from top to bottom, and of new officers for the lower, middle and upper echelons of the Hungarian Workers' Party. These officers shall convoke a Party Congress as early as possible in order to elect a Central Committee . . .

5 We demand that general elections, by universal, secret ballot be held throughout the country to elect a new National Assembly, with all political parties participating. We demand that the right of the workers to strike be recognised . . .

12 We demand complete recognition of freedom of opinion and expression, of freedom of the press and radio . . .

15 The students of the Technological University of Budapest declare unanimously their solidarity with the workers and students of Warsaw and Poland in their movement towards national independence.

**Source B:** from a radio broadcast by Janos Kadar, 4 November 1956.

The Hungarian Revolutionary Worker-Peasant Government has been formed . . . Our socialist achievements, our people's State, our worker-peasant power and the very existence of our country has been threatened by the weakness of the Imre Nagy Government and the increased influence of the counter-revolutionary elements who edged their way into the movement. This has prompted us, as Hungarian patriots, to form the Hungarian Revolutionary Worker-Peasant Government.

The Hungarian Revolutionary Worker-Peasant Government, acting in the interest of our people, working class and country, requested the Soviet Army Command to help our nation smash the sinister forces of reaction and restore order and calm in our country.

**Source C:** from a television broadcast by President John F. Kennedy, 25 July 1961.

There is peace in Berlin today. The source of world trouble and tension is Moscow, not Berlin. And if war begins, it will have begun in Moscow and not Berlin.

For the choice of peace or war is largely theirs, not ours. It is the Soviets who have stirred up this crisis. It is they who are trying to force a change. It is they who have opposed free elections. It is they who have rejected an all-German peace treaty and the rulings of international law . . .

In short, while we are ready to defend our interests, we shall also be ready to search for peace—in quiet exploratory talks, in formal or informal meetings. We do not want military considerations to dominate the thinking of either East or West.

**Source D:** from a speech by Nikita Khrushchev on Soviet radio and television, 7 August 1961.

The question of access to West Berlin and the whole question of the peace treaty is for [the Western Powers] only a pretext. If we abandoned our intention of concluding a peace treaty, they would take this as a strategic breakthrough and would in no time broaden the range of their demands. They would demand the abolition of the socialist system in the German Democratic Republic. If they achieved this too, they would, of course, undertake to wrest from Poland and Czechoslovakia the lands that were restored to them under the Potsdam Agreement—and these are Polish and Czechoslovak lands. And if the Western powers achieved all this, they would come forward with their principal demand—that the socialist system be abolished in all the countries of the socialist camp. They would like this even now.

**Source E:** from Lyndon B. Johnson, *The Vantage Point: Perspectives of the Presidency* (1971).

I tried to think through what would happen to our nation and to the world—if we let South Vietnam fall to Hanoi . . .

This is what I could foresee. First, it seemed likely that all of Southeast Asia would pass under Communist control, slowly or quickly, but inevitably . . . On both sides of the line between Communist and non-Communist Asia the struggle for Vietnam and Laos was regarded as a struggle for the fate of Southeast Asia.

Second, I knew our people well enough to realise that if we walked away from Vietnam and let Southeast Asia fall, there would follow a divisive and destructive debate in our country . . . It would inevitably increase isolationist pressures from the right and the left and cause a pulling back from our commitments in Europe and the Middle East as well as in Asia . . .

Third, our allies not just in Asia but throughout the world would conclude that our word was worth little or nothing. Those who had counted so long for their security on American commitments would be deeply shaken and vulnerable . . .

Fourth, knowing what I did of the policies and actions of Moscow and Peking, I was sure . . . that if we did not live up to our commitment in Southeast Asia and elsewhere, they would move to exploit the disarray in the United States and in the alliances of the Free World . . . I knew they could not resist the opportunity to expand their control into the vacuum of power we would leave behind us.

**Source F:** from J.P.D. Dunbabin, *The Cold War* (1994).

In the 1960s, the USA had increased its involvement in Indo-China to prove that communist insurgency could be resisted and to demonstrate the credibility of its guarantees to its allies. It had failed on both counts, not as a result of military defeat, but because its will to fight had evaporated. There were many reasons for this. One was simply the length of the war . . .

From mid-1967, US administrations were operating against the background of a strident anti-war movement. This was clearly not strong enough to induce the US government to pull out of Vietnam; but it did have a significant effect . . . in deterring or limiting escalation. The desire to restore domestic calm was an important factor in encouraging the policy of "Vietnamisation", and the withdrawal of US ground forces . . .

The USA's Vietnam experience was traumatic. It led to some questioning of Cold War beliefs, and to a more widespread reluctance to risk further entanglements.

[*END OF SOURCES FOR SPECIAL TOPIC 12*]

1997

**SPECIAL TOPIC 13: IRELAND 1900–1985: A DIVIDED IDENTITY**

**Study the sources below and then answer the questions in the accompanying question paper.**

**Source A:** an Ulster Unionist poster, 1912.

**Source B:** from a description by Lord Dunleath, one of the organisers, of the formation of the Ulster Volunteer Force in 1913.

We felt that it was the plain duty of those of us who were possessed of influence to take some step which would convince the government of the reality of our determination to resist this policy by every means in our power . . . We commenced by drilling our Orangemen and our Unionist Clubs. Later on we amalgamated these forces, organised them into companies and battalions, appointed officers and section leaders, and gradually equipped and trained them into a fairly efficient force of volunteer infantry. Finally we succeeded in providing them with a good supply of arms and ammunition. We can certainly claim that we have succeeded in turning the attention of Englishmen and Scotchmen towards Ulster and its inhabitants; we can also claim that the existence of this large armed force of Volunteers has materially assisted our political leaders.

**Source C:** from P. Buckland, *James Craig* (1990).

Ulster Unionists professed themselves content with the status quo under the Union. They enjoyed being part of the Protestant majority of the United Kingdom and believed that Ireland had prospered under the Union. Most obviously, industry had flourished in the North East, where Belfast had established itself as the world's major linen centre and Harland & Wolff were producing by the early twentieth century the largest ships in the world . . . Moreover, Ulster Unionists were convinced that an Irish parliament would be dominated by lower-class Catholics and would be at the mercy of priests and agitators. Such a prospect appalled and terrified them, for they did not trust an Irish parliament so constituted to deal fairly with them. Home Rule, they predicted, would result in the removal of civil and religious liberty and in economic and social chaos.

**Source D:** from A. Birrell, *Things Past Redress* (1937). Birrell was Secretary for Ireland at the time of the Easter Rising.

As a "rebellion" it was a ridiculous failure from the first, but as an event in Irish history it was horrible and heartbreaking, and being accompanied by house-to-house fighting, sniping and murdering, it stains the memory. It was a supreme act of criminal folly on the part of those who were responsible for it, for it never had a chance, and was really nothing more than a Dublin row.

**Source E:** from a letter, Bishop Edward O'Dwyer to General Maxwell, British Army Commander in Ireland, 1916.

You took care that no pleas of mercy should interpose on behalf of the poor young fellows who surrendered to you in Dublin.

The first information which we got of their fate was the announcement that they had been shot in cold blood. Personally, I regard your action with horror, and I believe it has outraged the conscience of the country. Then the deporting of hundreds and even thousands of poor fellows without trial of any kind seems to me an abuse of power as stupid as it is arbitrary, and altogether your regime has been one of the worst and blackest chapters in the history of the misgovernment of the country.

**Source F:** from *An t-Oglach*, the newspaper of the Irish Volunteers, 31 January 1918.

The principal means at the command of the Irish people is the Army of Ireland, and that army will be true to its trust . . . If they are called upon to shed blood in defence of the new-born Republic, they will not shrink from the sacrifice . . .

Dail Eireann . . . declares a "state of war" to exist between Ireland and England . . .; it further declares that that state of war can never be ended until the English military invader evacuates our country . . .

The state of war . . . justifies Irish Volunteers in treating the armed forces of the enemy—whether soldiers or policemen—exactly as a National Army would treat the members of an invading army.

Every volunteer is entitled, morally and legally . . . to use all legitimate methods of warfare against the soldiers and policemen of the English usurper, and to slay them if necessary to do so in order to overcome their resistance.

**Source G:** from *The Bold Black and Tan*, a song popular in Ireland in 1920.

The town of Balbriggan they've burned to the ground
While bullets like hailstones were whizzing around;
And women left homeless by this evil clan.
They've waged war on children, the bold Black and Tan.

Ah, then not by the terrors of England's foul horde,
For ne'er could a nation be ruled by the sword;
For our country we'll have yet in spite of her plan
Or ten times the number of bold Black and Tan.

We've defeated conscription in spite of their threats,
And we're going to defeat old Lloyd George and his pets;
For Ireland and Freedom we're here to a man,
And we'll humble the pride of the bold Black and Tan.

**Source H:** from the chapter by D. Fitzpatrick in R.F. Foster (ed.), *The Oxford History of Ireland* (1992).

The slide towards terrorism was largely precipitated by increasingly brutal repression which forced armed Volunteers to "go on the run" and band together for protection. After the reintroduction of massive internment under the Restoration of Order in Ireland Act (August 1920), these groups began to crystallise as "flying columns" plotting ambushes against enemy parties . . . The three or four thousand armed activists had no practical hope of military victory, yet their defiant survival frustrated the army and police and increased pressure for a truce and settlement.

The rapid intensification of violence after 1919 was largely caused by the disorganisation and savagery of the "occupying" forces. The worst atrocities were committed not by the army, but by the reconstituted Royal Irish Constabulary, which was swamped in 1920 by ex-soldiers enrolled as special constables or "Black and Tans", as well as "auxiliary cadets" who were recruited from the wartime officer corps . . . The militaristic nature of Irish government between 1916 and 1919 was superseded in 1920–1921 by a savage and calculated chaos which shattered the remains of the pre-war Anglo-Irish state.

[*END OF SOURCES FOR SPECIAL TOPIC 13*]

[*END OF SOURCES*]

SCOTTISH CERTIFICATE OF EDUCATION 1997

WEDNESDAY, 14 MAY
1.00 PM – 3.00 PM

# HISTORY HIGHER GRADE
## Paper II
## Questions

### SPECIAL TOPIC 1: NORMAN CONQUEST AND EXPANSION 1050–1153

**Answer *all* of the following questions.** *Marks*

1. Why did William, Duke of Normandy, invade England in 1066? Refer to **Source A** in your answer. **6**

2. How far does the evidence in **Source B** support the view that the success of William's invasion was mainly due to the activities of Tostig? **7**

3. In what ways do Brown and Sayles (**Sources C** and **D**) disagree about the appearance of feudalism in England? **5**

4. How well does **Source E** illustrate the value of feudalism to the crown? **5**

5. To what extent did Anglo-Saxon society and government survive the Norman Conquest? Refer to **Sources C**, **D**, **E** and **F** in your answer. **8**

6. To what extent do **Sources G** and **H** explain the differences between the "Norman" takeovers of England and Scotland? **7**

7. How accurate is it to say that there was a single Norman achievement in Europe? **7**

**(45)**

[*END OF QUESTIONS ON SPECIAL TOPIC 1*]

## SPECIAL TOPIC 2: THE CRUSADES 1096–1204

**Answer *all* of the following questions.** *Marks*

**1.** How well does **Source A** illustrate the underlying causes of the crusades? **6**

**2.** In what ways do Mayer (**Source B**) and Riley-Smith (**Source C**) differ in their views of the People's Crusade? **4**

**3.** Why did the People's Crusade fail? Refer to **Source B** in your answer. **6**

**4.** Explain why **Sources D** and **E** differ in their views of Bohemond. **5**

**5.** To what extent do **Sources D, E** and **F** support the view that Raymond represented the crusading ideal more closely than Bohemond? **8**

**6.** How well does **Source G** explain the effect of the crusades on the Moslems? **5**

**7.** How useful is **Source H** in explaining why the crusaders succeeded in capturing Jerusalem? **5**

**8.** What were the main social and political effects of the crusades on Europe? **6**

**(45)**

[*END OF QUESTIONS ON SPECIAL TOPIC 2*]

## SPECIAL TOPIC 3: TRADE AND TOWNS

**Answer *all* of the following questions.**

**1.** In what ways does the plan of Stirling (**Source A**) support the views of Ewan in **Source B**? **6**

**2.** How far do **Sources C** and **D** indicate that merchants did not exclude craftsmen from burgh government in the fourteenth century? **6**

**3.** To what extent was urban unrest in fourteenth-century Europe caused by quarrels between merchants and craftsmen? **6**

**4.** What light does **Source F** throw on the changes in burgh government between the twelfth and fourteenth centuries? **5**

**5.** How well do **Sources A, D, E** and **F** explain how burghs were developing an independent sense of community? **8**

**6.** How fully does **Source G** illustrate the range of functions of the guild? **7**

**7.** Were trade and towns in decline in fifteenth-century Scotland? Refer to **Source H** in your answer. **7**

**(45)**

[*END OF QUESTIONS ON SPECIAL TOPIC 3*]

1997

## SPECIAL TOPIC 4: SCOTLAND 1689–1715

**Answer *all* of the following questions.** *Marks*

1. How well does **Source A** explain the course of relations between Scotland and England from 1689 to 1707? 6

2. How fully do **Sources B** and **C** set out the case against the proposed Union? 6

3. How widely held at the time were the opinions expressed in **Source C**? 4

4. In what ways and for what reasons do **Sources B** and **D** differ about the possible consequences of Union? 6

5. Assess the value of **Source E** as historical evidence. 4

6. How well do **Sources F** and **G** explain the part played by the "New Party" (*Squadrone Volante*) in the negotiations leading to Union? 6

7. To what extent do you accept **Source F**'s analysis of the motives of the politicians involved in the Union debate? 5

8. To what extent did the immediate impact of the Union to 1714 confirm the arguments of **Sources B, C** and **D**? 8

**(45)**

[*END OF QUESTIONS ON SPECIAL TOPIC 4*]

## SPECIAL TOPIC 5: THE ATLANTIC SLAVE TRADE

**Answer *all* of the following questions.**

1. How useful is **Source A** as evidence of slave resistance to the slave trade? 4

2. To what extent did slave revolts in the New World affect the abolitionists' campaigns in Britain? 5

3. How fully do **Sources B** and **C** illustrate the methods used by abolitionists to influence public opinion? 7

4. Were the arguments in **Source D** typical of the attitudes of religious people towards slavery and the slave trade? 4

5. How well does the evidence in **Source D** support Walvin's argument in **Source C**? 5

6. To what extent does **Source E** illustrate the economic importance of the slave trade to Britain? 5

7. Why did the arguments in **Source E** receive more support in Parliament than those in **Source D** before 1806? 7

8. Why was the slave trade abolished in 1807? Refer to **Sources C, D, F** and **G** in your answer. 8

**(45)**

[*END OF QUESTIONS ON SPECIAL TOPIC 5*]

## SPECIAL TOPIC 6: THE AMERICAN REVOLUTION

**Answer *all* of the following questions.** *Marks*

1. Does **Source A** or Mr Harris in **Source B** describe more accurately British colonial control in America in the 1760s and early 1770s? **6**
2. Explain the significance of **Source C** in the context of events at the time. **4**
3. Explain fully the attitude towards the Crown expressed in **Source D**. **6**
4. Why did the Americans declare their independence within a year of writing **Source D**? **5**
5. How typical of British opinion were the views expressed in **Source E** towards American independence? **5**
6. How fully do **Sources A, B, C** and **E** illustrate the issues which led to the war of independence? **8**
7. How successfully did the Constitution of 1787 deal with these issues? **5**
8. To what extent do **Sources F** and **G** explain British defeat in the war of independence? **6**

**(45)**

[*END OF QUESTIONS ON SPECIAL TOPIC 6*]

## SPECIAL TOPIC 7: THE ENLIGHTENMENT IN SCOTLAND

**Answer *all* of the following questions.**

1. Compare the views of change in the Highlands in **Sources A** and **B**. **5**
2. How typical were the activities described in **Sources C** and **D** of Scottish intellectual life during the Enlightenment? **7**
3. How well does **Source C** illustrate the influence of science on agricultural improvement in eighteenth-century Scotland? **5**
4. Assess the connection between the Enlightenment and social life in Edinburgh. Refer to **Source D** in your answer. **4**
5. How useful is **Source E** as evidence of the importance of architecture in eighteenth-century Scotland? **5**
6. To what extent does Carlyle (**Source F**) explain the causes of the Scottish Enlightenment? **6**
7. How important to the Enlightenment were the connections with Europe described in **Source G**? **5**
8. How significant were the professions to the development of the Scottish Enlightenment? Refer to **Sources C, F** and **G** in your answer. **8**

**(45)**

[*END OF QUESTIONS ON SPECIAL TOPIC 7*]

## SPECIAL TOPIC 8: PATTERNS OF MIGRATION: SCOTLAND 1830s–1930s

**Answer *all* of the following questions.** *Marks*

1. To what extent are the views in **Source A** supported by the evidence in **Source B**? 6
2. How useful is **Source C** as evidence of attitudes towards Irish immigrants in Scotland at the time? 6
3. For what reasons did Irish and Highland migrants move to urban areas of Scotland during the period 1830s–1880s? 6
4. To what extent do you accept the views about the clergy in **Source D**? 6
5. How accurate is Devine's analysis (**Source E**) of differences between the ways of life of Highland and Irish migrants to Scottish cities? 6
6. How significant were the effects of migration on education in Scotland during the period 1830s–1880s? Refer to **Sources C, F** and **G** in your answer. 8
7. Assess the impact on Scottish life of emigration from Scotland during the period 1830s–1930s. 7

**(45)**

[*END OF QUESTIONS ON SPECIAL TOPIC 8*]

## SPECIAL TOPIC 9: THE THIRD FRENCH REPUBLIC 1871–1914

**Answer *all* of the following questions.**

1. How valuable is **Source A** as evidence about the purposes of Ferry's educational reforms? 5
2. How important was education in the debate about relations between Church and State under the Third Republic? Refer to **Sources A, B** and **C** in your answer. 8
3. To what extent does the evidence in **Source D** support the assessment of the Ralliement in **Source E**? 6
4. How successful was the change in Church policy towards the state outlined in **Source D**? 6
5. How justified were the fears expressed by Dupuy in **Source F**? 6
6. To what extent would you accept Cobban's evaluation (**Source G**) of the achievements of the Third Republic? 7
7. Why was France able to end her diplomatic isolation by 1905? 7

**(45)**

[*END OF QUESTIONS ON SPECIAL TOPIC 9*]

## SPECIAL TOPIC 10: AFRICAN SOCIETIES AND EUROPEAN IMPERIALISM 1880–1914

**Answer *all* of the following questions.** *Marks*

1. How far does the evidence in **Source A** about the motives of Europeans in the colonisation of Africa support the views expressed in **Source B**? 5
2. Explain why you consider **Source A** to be reliable **or** unreliable as historical evidence. 4
3. How important were commercial interests in the British occupation of Egypt in 1882? 5
4. How fully does **Source C** explain British policy towards East Africa before 1890? 6
5. To what extent does the evidence in **Source D** support the historian's views in **Source E**? 6
6. How well does **Source G** illustrate the effects of colonisation on native Africans? 6
7. "We've come to trade !!" they said (**Source G**). How far does this explain European colonisation of West Africa? 5
8. How important a part did religion play in European imperialism in Africa? Refer to **Sources D, F** and **G** in your answer. 8

**(45)**

[*END OF QUESTIONS ON SPECIAL TOPIC 10*]

## SPECIAL TOPIC 11: APPEASEMENT AND THE ROAD TO WAR, TO 1939

**Answer *all* of the following questions.**

1. How well does **Source A** explain the issues facing the British government when Germany reoccupied the Rhineland? 6
2. To what extent do you accept **Source B**'s analysis of the Rhineland crisis? 6
3. To what extent did the views expressed in **Source C** influence British policy towards Nazi aggression during the years 1937–1939? 6
4. Compare the views on the Anschluss given in **Sources D** and **E**. 5
5. How useful is **Source D** as evidence about the development of the policy of appeasement in the late 1930s? 4
6. ". . . series of humiliating diplomatic defeats . . . ever since 1931." How far do you agree with this claim by Fletcher in **Source E**? 6
7. Explain the significance of **Source F** in the context of events at the time. 4
8. How justified was the policy of appeasement? Refer to **Sources A, F** and **G** in your answer. 8

**(45)**

[*END OF QUESTIONS ON SPECIAL TOPIC 11*]

## SPECIAL TOPIC 12: THE ORIGINS AND DEVELOPMENT OF THE COLD WAR 1945–1985

**Answer *all* of the following questions.**

*Marks*

1. What can be learned from **Source A** about the reform movement in Hungary in 1956? **4**

2. Why did the views expressed in **Source A** cause such concern at the time in the USSR? **5**

3. How fully does **Source B** explain the actions taken by the Soviet Union to suppress the Hungarian uprising? **6**

4. Compare the views in **Sources C** and **D** on the situation in Berlin in 1961. **5**

5. How well does Khrushchev (**Source D**) explain the attitude of the Soviet Union to the issue of Berlin? **5**

6. How far do you accept President Johnson's arguments in **Source E** in favour of United States involvement in Vietnam? **6**

7. How accurate is Dunbabin's analysis (**Source F**) of the impact of the Vietnam war on American foreign policy? **6**

8. How significant were ideological factors in the development of the Cold War from the mid 1950s to 1970? Refer to **Sources A, B, D** and **E** in your answer. **8**

**(45)**

[*END OF QUESTIONS ON SPECIAL TOPIC 12*]

## SPECIAL TOPIC 13: IRELAND 1900–1985: A DIVIDED IDENTITY

**Answer *all* of the following questions.**

1. Discuss the significance of **Source A** in the light of events at the time. **4**

2. To what extent did the attitudes expressed in **Sources B** and **C** represent a serious challenge to the authority of the British government? **6**

3. How fully does **Source C** explain the hostility of Ulster Protestants towards Home Rule? **6**

4. To what extent do you accept Birrell's views (**Source D**) on the Easter Rising? **5**

5. How reliable is **Source E** as evidence of Irish opinion on the British suppression of the Easter Rising? **5**

6. How well does **Source F** illustrate the development of the nationalist campaign against British forces in Ireland? **5**

7. To what extent does **Source G** support the views of the historian Fitzpatrick in **Source H**? **6**

8. Explain why there was tension between the majority of the Irish people and the British government between 1916 and 1921. Refer to **Sources E, F, G** and **H** in your answer. **8**

**(45)**

[*END OF QUESTIONS ON SPECIAL TOPIC 13*]

[*END OF QUESTION PAPER*]

SCOTTISH CERTIFICATE OF EDUCATION 1998

THURSDAY, 14 MAY
9.30 AM – 11.30 AM

# HISTORY HIGHER GRADE
## Paper I

### OPTION A: MEDIEVAL HISTORY

**Answer THREE questions selected from at least two Sections, one of which must be Section (a).**

#### Section (a): Medieval Society

1. How true is it to say that castles were only important as status symbols for their owners?

2. How consistent were patterns of settlement and field systems across Scotland?

3. Do you agree that in the twelfth century it was the economic and social activities of the regular and secular church which had most impact on the common folk?

4. Did Henry II's work on the development of law, order and justice do more than copy the work of Henry I?

5. To what extent were Henry II's problems in controlling the Angevin empire due to the activities of his sons?

#### Section (b): Nation and King

6. To what extent was Magna Carta the response of the barons to the growing concentration of power in the hands of the Angevin monarchy?

7. How effectively did Philip II assert his authority as king of France?

8. Was it his piety or his policies which made Louis IX a successful monarch?

9. "Robert Bruce seized the throne for his own personal satisfaction and not for the good of Scotland." Discuss.

#### Section (c): Crisis of Authority

10. How far was France damaged economically, socially and politically by the Hundred Years' War?

11. To what extent did the Black Death merely accelerate social and economic changes which were taking place already in early fourteenth-century Europe?

12. Is it true to say that the Peasants' Revolt of 1381 was aimless and disorganised?

13. How far did the Conciliar Movement solve the problems which faced the papacy in the fourteenth and fifteenth centuries?

## OPTION B: EARLY MODERN HISTORY

**Answer THREE questions selected from at least two Sections, one of which must be Section (a).**

### Section (a): Scotland and England in the Century of Revolutions (1603–1702)

**1.** Were financial difficulties the most important threat to royal authority in England before 1629?

**2.** Why did so many people sign the Covenant of 1638?

**3.** Did the governments of 1649–1660 rely too heavily on military support to be successful?

**4.** Did the social groups which brought about the Revolution of 1688–1689 benefit most from it?

**5.** How important was the personal influence of the monarchs in the politics of seventeenth-century Britain?

### Section (b): Royal Authority in 17th and 18th Century Europe

**6.** Compare the effectiveness of central and local government under Louis XIV.

**7.** How important was the Revocation of the Edict of Nantes to the establishment of Louis XIV's absolutism?

**8.** Did Joseph II's enlightened ideals lead him to try to do too much too quickly?

**9.** What were the social effects of the policies of Joseph II?

### Section (c): The French Revolution: The Emergence of the Citizen State

**10.** To what extent were state and society in conflict under the Ancien Régime?

**11.** "Enlightened ideas would not have undermined royal authority without the financial problems of the monarchy." How far is this true of France in the 1780s?

**12.** How important was the personal role of Louis XVI in the development of the French Revolution between 1789 and 1793?

**13.** How far were French governments from 1793 to 1799 concerned with re-establishing authority?

1998

## OPTION C: LATER MODERN HISTORY

**Answer THREE questions selected from at least two Sections, one of which must be Section (a).**

### Section (a): Britain 1850s–1979

**1.** "By 1928 the essentials of democracy had been achieved." How far would you agree?

**2.** How important was the contribution of the socialist societies to the growth of the Labour Movement in Britain up to 1914?

**3.** To what extent did the Liberal Government (1906–1914) set up a welfare state in Britain?

**4.** "Too little, too late." Is this a fair judgement on the social and economic measures of the National Government, 1931–1939?

**5.** Explain the varying electoral fortunes of the Scottish National Party during the period 1945–1979.

### Section (b): The Growth of Nationalism

**6.** How would you explain the lack of success of the nationalist movement in **either** Germany **or** Italy during the period 1815–1860?

**7.** "A country united in name only." How far would you agree with this judgement on **either** Germany **or** Italy during the period 1871–1914?

**8.** Assess the importance of economic factors in the rise to power of **either** the Nazi Party in Germany between 1918 and 1933 **or** the Fascist Party in Italy between 1918 and 1924.

**9.** How far did the Fascist state rely on fear rather than popular support for its survival? Discuss with reference **either** to Germany 1933–1939 **or** Italy 1922–1939.

## Section (c): The Large Scale State

### Answer on the USA OR Russia OR China

*The USA*

**10.** "An increasing resentment and hostility." To what extent is this an accurate description of American attitudes towards immigration in the years after 1918?

**11.** "Success on the surface, problems underneath." How far would you agree with this analysis of the policies of the Republican administrations of the 1920s?

**12.** To what extent did the economic problems of the 1930s cause a growth in the powers of the Federal Government?

**13.** Explain why there was growing pressure for civil rights in the period 1945–1960.

**OR**

*Russia*

**14.** How far did industrialisation present a challenge to the authority of the Tsarist state before 1905?

**15.** "Any changes were more apparent than real." Is this an accurate analysis of the structure of the Tsarist state in the years following the 1905 Revolution?

**16.** Why did the Provisional Government fail to retain power in Russia in 1917?

**17.** To what extent was the victory of the Red Army in the Civil War due to its superior organisation and leadership?

**OR**

*China*

**18.** Why was the Revolution of 1911–1912 followed by years of political instability in China?

**19.** To what extent did the May the Fourth Movement lead to the development of national feeling in China in the 1920s?

**20.** Why did the Communist Party succeed in achieving power in China in 1949?

**21.** To what extent was the death of Mao followed by major changes in Chinese government policy?

[*END OF QUESTION PAPER*]

SCOTTISH CERTIFICATE OF EDUCATION 1998

THURSDAY, 14 MAY
1.00 PM – 3.00 PM

# HISTORY
## HIGHER GRADE
### Paper II
### Sources

| *Option* | *Special Topic* |
|---|---|
| **A Medieval History** | 1 Norman Conquest and Expansion 1050–1153 |
| | 2 The Crusades 1096–1204 |
| | 3 Trade and Towns |
| **B Early Modern History** | 4 Scotland 1689–1715 |
| | 5 The Atlantic Slave Trade |
| | 6 The American Revolution |
| | 7 The Enlightenment in Scotland |
| **C Later Modern History** | 8 Patterns of Migration: Scotland 1830s–1930s |
| | 9 The Third French Republic 1871–1914 |
| | 10 African Societies and European Imperialism 1880–1914 |
| | 11 Appeasement and the Road to War, to 1939 |
| | 12 The Origins and Development of the Cold War 1945–1985 |
| | 13 Ireland 1900–1985: a Divided Identity |

1998

## SPECIAL TOPIC 1: NORMAN CONQUEST AND EXPANSION 1050–1153

**Study the sources below and then answer the questions in the accompanying question paper.**

**Source A:** from *The Deeds of William, Duke of the Normans and King of the English,* written *c.*1071 by William of Poitiers, describing an assembly held by Duke William in Normandy.

The duke strengthened the resolve of the alarmists with the following speech: "We all know," he said, "the cleverness of Harold. He may inspire fear, but he also raises our hopes. He dispenses his wealth to no effect, wasting his gold without strengthening his position. He does not dare to promise the least part of what belongs to me. I, however, shall promise and give away as I please those possessions which are now said to be his equally with those that are mine at present. Without doubt he who is prepared to bestow not only his own property but that of his foe, will overcome. The lack of a fleet shall be no hindrance to us for we shall soon possess sufficient ships . . . wars are won by courage rather than the number of soldiers. Furthermore, Harold will fight to keep what he has unjustly seized; we seek what has been given to us, which we have gained in return for the services we have rendered."

**Source B:** from *The Deeds of William, Duke of the Normans and King of the English,* written *c.*1071 by William of Poitiers.

This Odo, bishop of Bayeux, was known to excel in affairs both ecclesiastical and secular. In the first place, his goodness and prudence is witnessed by the church of Bayeux which with great zeal he set in good order and embellished, for though yet young in years he was more mature in capacity than older men . . . Next, he served all Normandy and added distinction to it . . . His love of justice merited no less praise. He never took up arms, nor ever wished to; yet he struck fear in the hearts of warriors . . . Normans and Bretons alike willingly served him as an ideal lord. Nor were the English such barbarians that they could not see well enough that this prelate, this governor, was to be feared but also to be revered and esteemed . . . Odo bishop of Bayeux and William fitz Osbern laudably performed their respective stewardships in the kingdom. Sometimes they acted singly and sometimes together . . . Also the local governors, each placed in a castle, zealously administered their districts.

**Source C:** from the *Ecclesiastical History* of Orderic Vitalis, written between *c.*1114 and 1141.

But meanwhile the English were groaning under the Norman yoke, and suffering oppressions from the proud lords who ignored the king's injunctions. The petty lords who were guarding the castles oppressed all the native inhabitants of high and low degree, and heaped shameful burdens on them. For Bishop Odo and William fitz Osbern, the king's vice-regents, were so swollen with pride that they would not deign to hear the reasonable plea of the English or give them impartial judgement. When their men-at-arms were guilty of plunder and rape they protected them by force, and wreaked the wrath all the more violently upon those who complained of the cruel wrongs they suffered.

**Source D:** from S. Reynolds, *Fiefs and Vassals* (1994).

The Normans seem to have been accustomed to fewer taxes and probably less formal military duties, and to a closer link between property rights and jurisdictions, than were the English, but there is not much evidence that the conquest changed fundamental ideas about the rights and obligations of property in England very much . . .

If, as long tradition asserts, feudalism was introduced to England by the Norman Conquest, then, whether it is seen in military terms as a matter of knights' fees and knight service or in jurisdictional terms as a matter of Lords' courts, it was a pretty brief affair which barely outlasted its first century . . . The introduction of the word fief and a new concept of the hierarchy of property rights seem to be genuine consequences of the conquest . . . The very word hierarchy may, however, be misleading: property rights were arranged in layers, but the top layer did not have most rights. Most of the rights of property, including the fundamental rights to use, management, and receipt of the income, were enjoyed, as they were elsewhere, by those at the lowest layer above that of the unfree peasants.

Properties that were called fiefs or fees in England fit the pattern of classic feudalism only in the roughest of ways. *Feudum* in England did not mean knight's fee any more than it did in France. It meant all free and heritable property.

**Source E:** from R.A. Brown, *Origins of English Feudalism* (1973).

The fee is a parcel of land held by a knight as the vassal and tenant of his lord, in return for military service (the crucial service among others) and more specifically military knight-service, to that lord . . . The very words feudal and feudalism are derived from the Latin *feudum* meaning fief (or fee). We may begin therefore by noting that the word *feudum* does not appear in England until after 1066 . . .

We thus reach an end. The fundamentals of feudalism—the knight, vassalic commendation, the fief, the castle—all of them are absent from the indigenous society, whether Anglo-Saxon or Scandinavian, of pre-Conquest England, and all are increasingly manifest after 1066. The origins of English feudalism, therefore, are found in the Norman Conquest.

**Source F:** from *The Deeds of William, Duke of the Normans and King of the English,* written *c.*1071 by William of Poitiers.

In 1067, in the castles William placed capable custodians, brought over from France, in whose loyalty no less than ability he trusted, together with large numbers of horse and foot. He distributed rich fiefs amongst them, in return for which they would willingly undertake hardships and dangers. But to no Frenchman was there given anything unjustly taken from an Englishman.

**Source G:** from R. Bartlett, *The Making of Europe* (1994).

There were clear advantages to be gained from enlisting warriors from other domains. Such men would be, initially at least, entirely dependent on the prince they served. They would have no local aristocratic or territorial ties to complicate their loyalties or to provide them with the capacity to be rivals . . . In areas such as Scotland or the West Slav lands, however, these general considerations were reinforced by specific ones: here the incomers brought superior techniques of war. This explains the coming of the Anglo-Normans to Scotland and the role of German settlers in Poland, Bohemia, Hungary and other parts of eastern Europe in the twelfth to fourteenth centuries.

[*END OF SOURCES FOR SPECIAL TOPIC 1*]

1998

## SPECIAL TOPIC 2: THE CRUSADES 1096–1204

**Study the sources below and then answer the questions in the accompanying question paper.**

**Source A:** from R. Bartlett, *The Making of Europe* (1994).

Recent work by German and French historians has suggested that the structure of the aristocratic family itself underwent a transformation in the tenth and eleventh centuries. Loosely linked kindreds . . . were replaced by clearly defined lineages, in which family lands and primogeniture became ever more important. A single line of male descent came to dominate at the expense of the wider kindred of the earlier period. If this picture is credible, it is possible that the expansionism of the eleventh, twelfth and thirteenth centuries was one result. The decline in opportunities for some members of the military aristocracy—notoriously, of course, younger sons—may have been the impetus to emigration. Indeed, one distinguished historian has seen the appeal of Scotland for immigrant knights in the twelfth century in the fact that it was "a land for younger sons"; while a leading historian of the Crusader States describes the knightly immigration to the Holy Land as "the work of younger sons or of young men".

**Source B:** from J. Riley-Smith, *The Crusades* (1990).

There is very little evidence to support the proposition that the first crusade was an opportunity for spare sons to make themselves scarce in order to relieve the family of burdens, or for landless knights to seek an easy way to make a fortune for themselves overseas . . .

This makes it difficult for me to believe that most crusaders, or at least most crusading knights, were motivated by crude materialism. The selling of property to invest in the fairly remote possibility of gaining land after a 2,000-mile march to the East would have been a stupid gamble . . . It makes much more sense to suppose that they, and especially their families, were moved by idealism. This was an age of ostentatious and extravagant generosity and monasteries and religious communities benefited greatly from it.

**Source C:** from *A History of the Expedition to Jerusalem* by Fulcher of Chartres, written between *c.*1101 and 1127.

The Franks entered the city [Jerusalem] magnificently at the noonday hour on Friday, the day of the week when Christ redeemed the whole world on the cross. With trumpets sounding and with everything in an uproar, exclaiming "Help, God!" they vigorously pushed into the city, and straightway raised the banner on top of the wall.

Count Raymond and his men, who were bravely assailing the city in another section, did not perceive this until they saw the Saracens jumping from the top of the wall. Seeing this, they joyfully ran to the city as quickly as they could, and helped the others pursue and kill the wicked enemy.

After they had discovered the cleverness of the Saracens, it was an extraordinary thing to see our squires and poorer people split the bellies of those dead Saracens, so that they might pick out gold coins from their intestines, which they had swallowed down their horrible gullets while alive. After several days, they made a great heap of their bodies and burned them to ashes, and in those ashes they found the gold more easily.

**Source D:** from the *Deeds of the Franks,* written between *c.*1098 and 1101.

We went on besieging Arqa for three months, all but one day, and celebrated Easter there on 10 April 1098. While the siege was going on, [Genoese] ships put into a port near at hand, and they were laden with plenty of provisions, corn, wine, meat, cheese, barley and oil, so that the whole army was very well supplied.

**Source E:** an extract about the siege of Acre, 1191, from *The Itinerary of Richard I*, written in the early thirteenth century.

The Pisans, wondering at Richard's magnificence and glory, came to him, offering their homage and fealty, and, of their own free will, binding themselves to his rule and service.

**Source F:** a map of the Mediterranean economy in the thirteenth century.

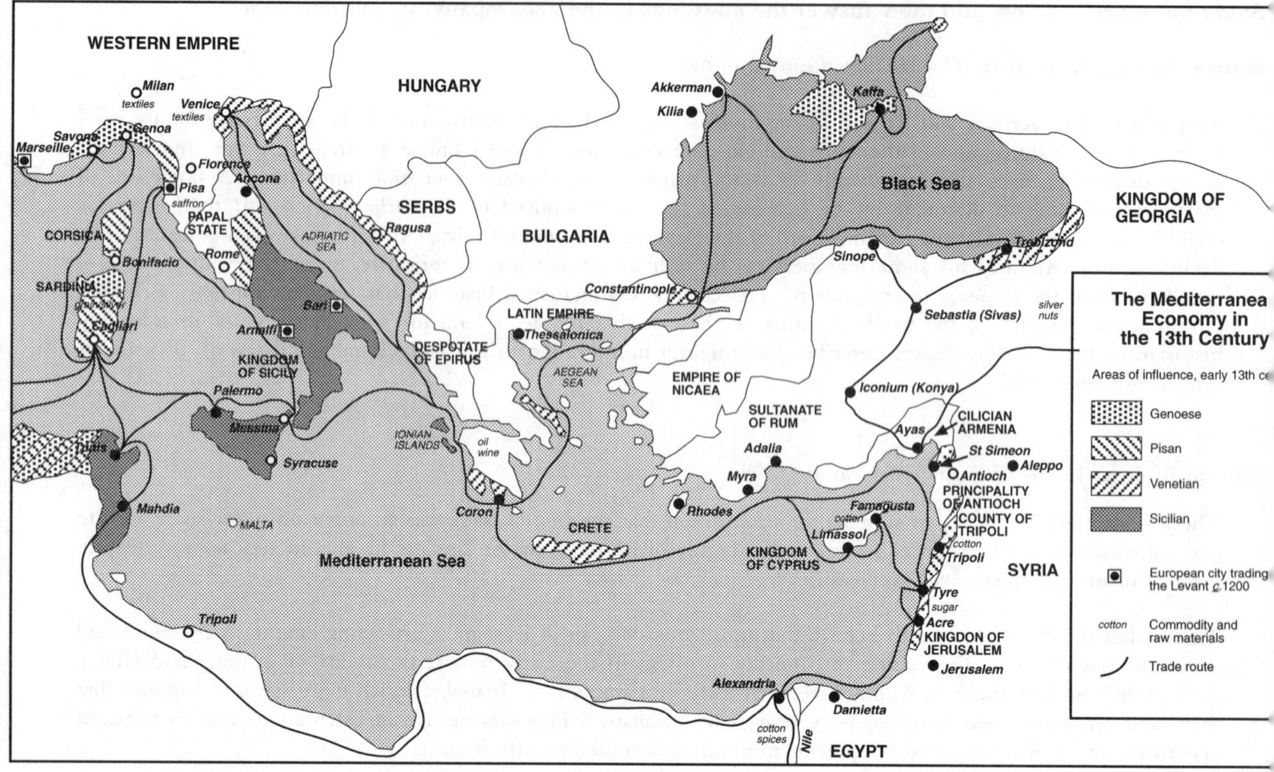


**Source G:** from Terry Jones and Alan Ereira, *Crusades* (1996).

> Saladin, utterly worn out, died five months after Richard left Acre. To some of his fellow countrymen he remained the Upstart, a man more prepared to fight his fellow-Moslems than the Franks and who used the rhetoric of *jihad* simply to fulfil his own ambitions. He brought Nur ed-Din's work to its logical conclusion by recapturing Jerusalem, but was criticized by his contemporaries for not being more ruthless with the Franks and for not driving them out of Palestine altogether. In the West, on the other hand, Saladin became an icon of chivalry. He was celebrated for his sense of honour, his generosity and his distaste for bloodshed.

**Source H:** negotiations with Saladin in 1191, from a biography of Saladin written *c.*1200 by Baha-ad-Din.

> On 3 November, the arrival was announced of the ambassador from Conrad of Montferrat.
>
> On 9 November the Sultan gave an audience and summoned Conrad's ambassador to hear his message and statement. He appeared with a whole group of companions—I was present at the audience—and Saladin treated him with great honour. He entered into conversation with him and had a sumptuous banquet served for them. After the meal he led them aside . . .
>
> That same night an ambassador came from the King of England: the son of Humphrey, one of the great Frankish leaders and kings. The Sultan sent for him and listened to what he had to say . . . When the audience was at an end and the Franks had gone, he turned to me and said, "When we have made peace with them, there will be nothing to prevent their attacking us treacherously. If I should die the Moslems would no longer be able to muster an army like this and the Franks would have the upper hand. It is better to carry on the Holy War until we have expelled them from Palestine, or death overtakes us". This was his opinion, and he only moved toward peace in response to external pressures.

[*END OF SOURCES FOR SPECIAL TOPIC 2*]

1998

## SPECIAL TOPIC 3: TRADE AND TOWNS

**Study the sources below and then answer the questions in the accompanying question paper.**

**Source A:** plan of Perth in the late twelfth century.

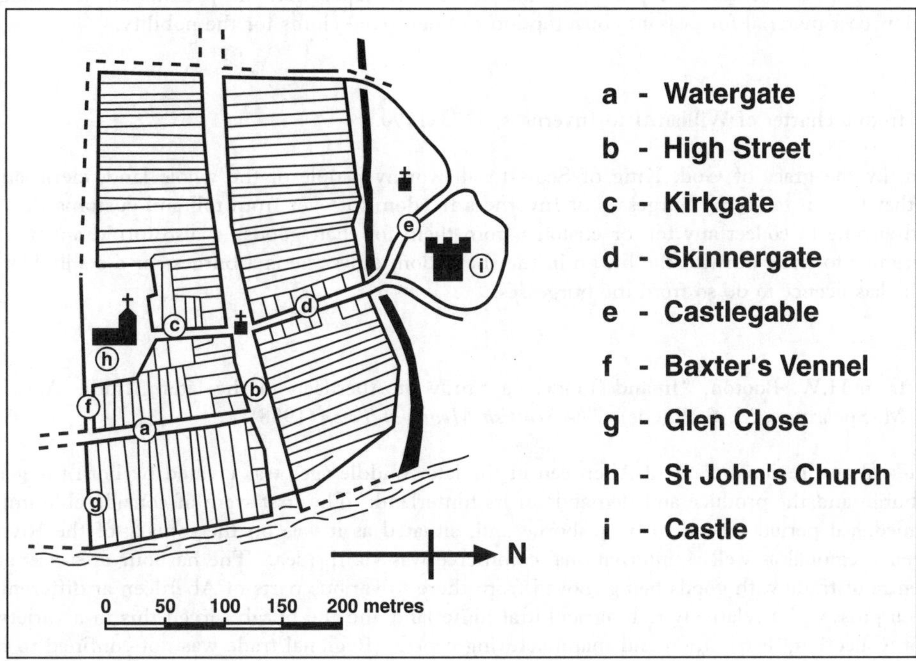


**Source B:** from a charter given by Alexander II to Elgin, 1234.

Alexander, by the grace of God, King of Scots, to all the worthy men of the whole land, greetings. Know that I grant and by this charter confirm to our burgesses at Elgin that they may have their merchant guild in the burgh. This should be for the benefit of the burgh. They should have their guild as freely as any of our burghs in the whole kingdom.

**Source C:** from a charter given by William I to Perth, *c.*1205x1210.

William, by the grace of God, King of Scots to all worthy men cleric and lay, greetings. I forbid any foreign merchant to buy or sell anything within the sheriffdom of Perth outside my burgh of Perth. But a foreign merchant may come to Perth and sell his merchandise there and invest his pennies. Any foreign merchants breaking this rule will be imprisoned.

Foreign merchants may only sell cloth in Perth between Ascension Day [five and a half weeks after Easter] and the first of August . . . and then they may sell cloth and other merchandise just as my burgesses do.

I order that all who live in Perth and wish to do business with my burgesses may do so at the market no matter whose men they are.

I grant that my burgesses of Perth may have their guild for merchants except for fullers and weavers. No one living in the sheriffdom of Perth, outwith the burgh of Perth, may make dyed cloth or motley apart from my burgesses who are in the merchant guild and share in paying my aids or those who have been granted this liberty by charter. No one in the sheriffdom outside the burgh may make dyed or shorn cloth under pain of my full forfeiture . . .

I forbid anyone from outwith the burgh of Perth to buy or sell hides or wool unless in my burgh of Perth . . .

**Source D:** from M. Lynch, *Scotland: a New History* (1992).

Urban industry was still limited and rudimentary, tied almost to animal-based products; much of it was based in the household, in a backyard rather than in a specialist workshop . . . Wool spawned a range of specialist occupations, such as fulling, waulking and weaving, but in the larger towns the complicated process was controlled, to their considerable profit, by the dyers who supervised the production of a range of cloth from rough, low cost material for peasant consumption to finer, dyed cloths for the nobility.

**Source E:** from a charter of William I to Inverness, 1173x1190.

William, by the grace of God, King of Scots to all worthy people of the whole land, cleric and lay, greetings. Know that I grant to all my burgesses of Inverness freedom for ever from toll and customs throughout my land. I forbid anyone to collect any toll or customs from them for their goods. I also forbid anyone to buy or sell in that burgh or to trade outwith the burgh in the sheriffdom unless he is a burgess or a stallholder in the burgh or unless he has licence to do so from the burgesses.

**Source F:** from H.W. Booton, "Inland Trade: a Study of Aberdeen in the later Middle Ages", in M. Lynch, M. Spearman, M. Stell (eds), *The Scottish Medieval Town* (1988).

The internal and regional trade of Aberdeen in the later middle ages was created by both the geographical assets of the burgh and the produce and demands of its hinterland. The first were of considerable importance. Trade in the medieval period tended to be seaborne and, situated as it was on the estuary of the River Dee, much of Aberdeen's regional as well as international commerce was via the sea. The harbour area was an important and busy centre of trade with goods being moved from there to various parts of Aberdeen at different rates of charge. Aberdeen possessed a relatively rich agricultural hinterland and the burgh served this in a variety of ways: as an entrepôt, collection, distribution and manufacturing centre. Regional trade was not confined to the sea, for there were substantial overland communications which must have represented a substantial but unknown percentage of regional commerce centred on Aberdeen. To help such inland trade there was to the north of the burgh a bridge over the River Don by the fourteenth century and by 1529 a bridge over the River Dee to the south of Aberdeen.

Aberdeen in the later middle ages enjoyed a flourishing domestic trade which was sophisticated in its structure and functioned at three levels: Aberdeen burgh, north-east regional and national.

**Source G:** map of the Dutch and Belgian coast in the late Middle Ages.

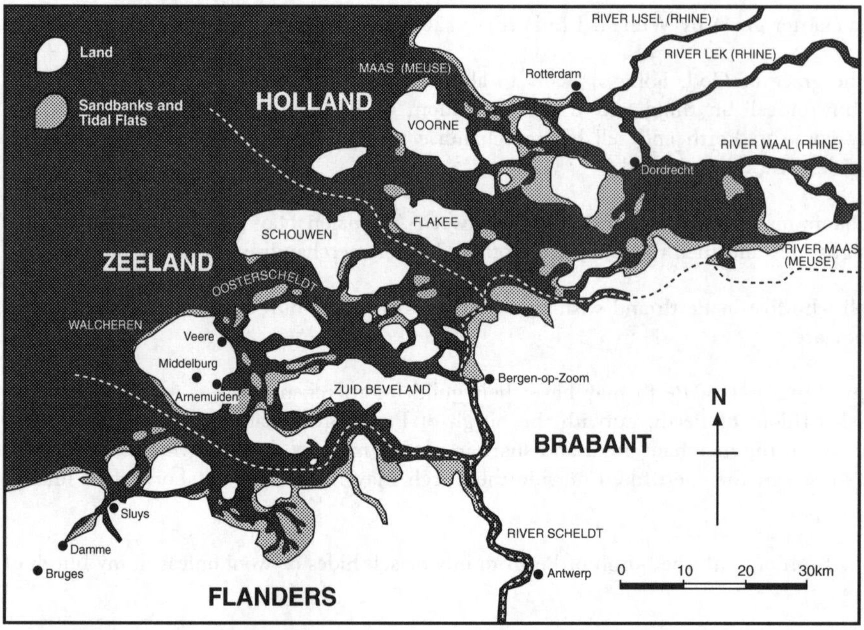

**Source H:** graphs of Scottish exports from 1327 to 1469, taken from exchequer rolls.

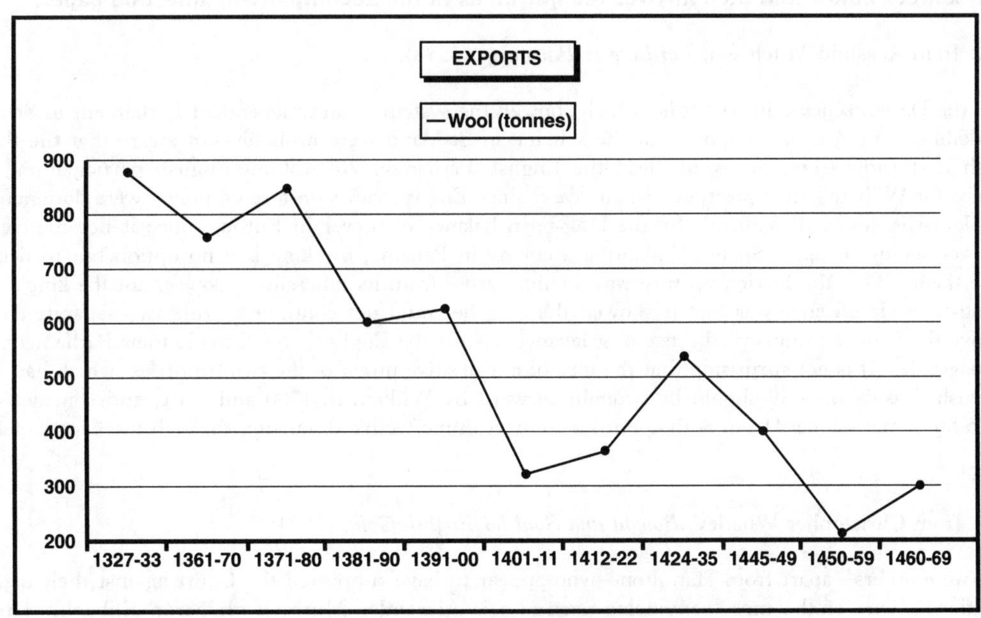


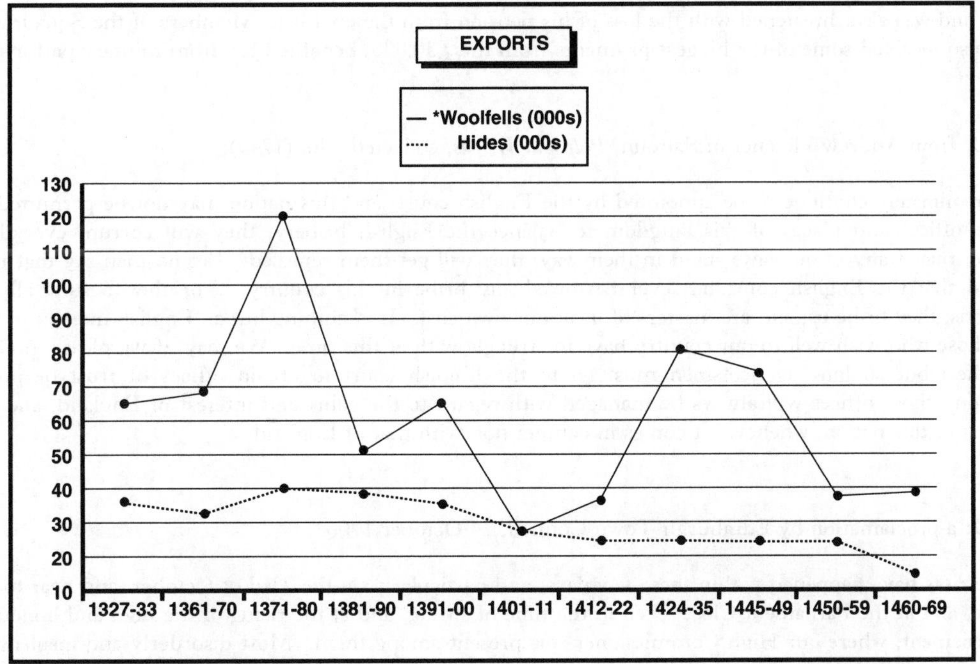


*Woolfells = unshorn sheepskins

[*END OF SOURCES FOR SPECIAL TOPIC 3*]

## SPECIAL TOPIC 4: SCOTLAND 1689–1715

**Study the sources below and then answer the questions in the accompanying question paper.**

**Source A:** from Rosalind Mitchison, *Lordship to Patronage* (1983).

It was the Darien scheme in particular which showed the system of an independent Parliament in Scotland to be unworkable. The original proposers of the scheme in Scotland were probably not aware that the threat to the English East India Company would lead the English Parliament to prohibit English participation. That was awkward for William's dual position. In any case, since English views on foreign policy were dominated by trade and colonial issues, and William's by the long-term balance of power in Europe, once it became clear that the Scots were going to upset Spain by planting a colony in Panama, the king had no option but to denounce and oppose them. That the Darien venture was a failure arose from its inherent weakness, not the king's opposition. Its long-term significance was that it showed the king he could not continue to rule two separate countries. It also gave the Scots an unjustified sense of grievance against the English, which made their Parliament even more unmanageable. It is not surprising that the idea of a legislative union of the two countries, which had been raised and brushed aside in 1689 should be brought forward by William in 1700 and 1701, and considered seriously enough for commissioners from both countries to meet in ineffective discussion through the winter of 1702–3.

**Source B:** from Christopher Whatley, *Bought and Sold for English Gold?* (1994).

There were others—apart from Hamilton—who appear to have supported the Court against their usual political inclinations. One of the most convincing examples is Alexander Murray, 4th baron Elibank. Other former opponents were Sir Kenneth Mackenzie of Cromartie, and the 11th earl of Glencairn, who received 100 pounds Scots and was also threatened with the loss of his pension from the civil list. Members of the Squadrone Volante, who also received some of the biggest payments from the £20,000, benefited too from military patronage.

**Source C:** from Andrew Fletcher of Saltoun, *Political Works*, collected edn. (1749).

If our ministers continue to be appointed by the English court, and this nation may not be permitted to dispose of the offices and places of this kingdom to balance the English bribery, they will corrupt everything to the degree, that if any of our laws stand in their way, they will get them repealed. Let no man say that it cannot be proved that the English court has ever bestowed any bribe in this country. For they bestow all offices and pensions; they bribe us, and are masters of us at our own cost. It is nothing but an English interest in this House, that those who wish well to our country have to struggle with at this time. We may, if we please, dream of other remedies; but so long as Scotsmen must go to the English court to obtain offices of trust or profit in this kingdom, those offices will always be managed with regard to the court and interest of England, and against the interest of this nation, whenever it comes in competition with that of England.

**Source D:** a proclamation by Edinburgh Town Council, 24 October 1706.

These riots have happened within these few days, and particularly on the 23rd of October, and near to Parliament House, and in the Parliament Close, even in the time of sitting, and at the rising of the high and honourable court of Parliament, where our High Commissioner was present among them. Most disorderly and insolent gatherings of commons filled the streets with clamour and confusion, and insulted not only peaceable persons but also some of the members of our high and honourable court of Parliament, presuming to threaten and invade them in their very dwelling houses, by a most villainous and outrageous mob.

**Source E:** from a speech by Lord Belhaven during the Union debates, reported by Daniel Defoe.

If the Lords Commissioners for England had been as civil and cooperative, they should certainly have finished a federal treaty likewise, that both nations might have the choice, which of them to have gone into, as they thought fit. But they would hear of nothing but an entire and complete Union, a name which means an Union, either by incorporation, surrender or conquest; whereas our Commissioners thought of nothing but a fair, equal Union.

**Source F:** from William Seton of Pitmedden, *A Speech in Parliament on the First Article of the Treaty of Union* (1706).

I could give some Account of the particular Advantages we'll obtain by an Incorporating Union with England, but there will be occasions to discuss these as the other Articles are considered by this Parliament. In general, I may assert, that by this Union, we'll have access to all the advantages in commerce the English enjoy. We'll be capable, by a good government, to improve our National Product, for the benefit of the whole island. And we'll have our liberty, property and religion secured under the protection of one Sovereign and one Parliament of Great Britain.

**Source G:** a section of a song written in a business book belonging to David Geddes, merchant, in 1709.

O Scotland awake
and get to your arms
for the English rogues have sworn
that you shall be brought down
down, down, down to the ground.

[*END OF SOURCES FOR SPECIAL TOPIC 4*]

1998

## SPECIAL TOPIC 5: THE ATLANTIC SLAVE TRADE

**Study the sources below and then answer the questions in the accompanying question paper.**

**Source A:** from evidence to a Parliamentary Commission on the slave trade *c*.1780.

It is the surgeon's business to go below every morning the first thing.

. . . Almost all the men slaves were taken ill with dysentery. I went down repeatedly amongst them. The last time that I went down it was so extremely hot that I took off my shirt. Upwards of twenty of them had fainted, or were fainting. I got several of them hauled upon deck, and two or three of them died, and most of the rest before I arrived in the West Indies. I think I had been down about fifteen minutes, and it made me so very ill that I could not get up without assistance. I was taken ill of a dysentery myself, and was unable to do my duty the whole passage afterwards.

**Source B:** from *The Travels of Mungo Park 1795–7* (1813).

Negroes are commonly secured by putting the right leg of one and the left of another into the same pair of fetters. By supporting the fetters with a string they can walk, though very slowly . . .

Such of them as show marks of discontent are secured in a different manner. A thick billet of wood is cut, about three feet long, and a smooth notch being made upon one side of it, the ankle of the slave is bolted to the smooth part by means of a strong iron staple, one prong of which passes on each side of the ankle . . .

In other respects, the treatment of the slaves during their stay at Kamalia was far from being harsh or cruel. They were led out in their fetters every morning to the shade of the tamarind tree, where they were encouraged to play at games of hazard, and sing diverting songs to keep up their spirits. Though some of them sustained the hardships of their situation with amazing fortitude, the greater part of them were very much dejected, and would sit all day in a kind of sullen melancholy, with their eyes fixed upon the ground. In the evening their irons were examined and their hand fetters put on, after which they were conducted into two large huts, where they were guarded during the night by Karfa's domestic slaves.

**Source C:** from the journal of John Newton, 26 April 1753.

I was at first continually alarmed with the slaves' almost desperate attempts to make attacks upon us . . . When most quiet they were always watching for an opportunity. However, from about the end of February they have behaved more like children in one family than slaves in chains and irons and are really upon all accounts more observant, obliging and considerate than our white people . . . It is true we are not wanting in such methods of guarding them as custom and prudence suggests, but I hope I shall never be weak and vain enough to think such a guard sufficient. "Except the Lord keep the city the watchman waketh but in vain." The same may be said of a ship in any circumstances and it is more observably true of a Guineaman.

**Source D:** from James Walvin, "Freeing the Slaves: How important was Wilberforce?" in J. Hayward (ed.), *Out of Slavery* (1985).

What made the anti-slavery case so convincing was the personal experience of those Methodist and Baptist missionaries, who were among the first to bring Christianity to West Indian slaves in the 1780s. Indeed, it was a fortuitous accident of timing that the anti-slave trade movement was founded when the first missionaries began to send back to Britain their own eye-witness accounts of the worst details of slave experience. Returning missionaries went on British lecture circuits, telling the chapel congregations of the sufferings of the slaves and of how the planters sought to prevent the conversion of slaves to Methodism and Baptism. It was bad enough to be a slave—but to be prevented from becoming a black methodist was to add religious insult to injury.

**Source E:** from a letter by William Wilberforce to the Rev. William Robertson, 25 January 1788.

What I have to request is that you will have the goodness to communicate to me such facts and observations as may be useful to me in the important task I have undertaken, of bringing forward into parliamentary discussion, the situation of that much injured part of the species, the poor Negroes.

The main object I have in view is the prevention of all further exports of slaves from Africa. [There are also other questions, including] their state in the West Indies, and the most practicable mode of improving it, the effects that might follow from this change of system in all its extended and complicated connections and relations, both in Africa and the Western World, and this not only in our own case but in those of other European nations, who might be induced to follow our example.

**Source F:** from G.F. Dow, *Slave Ships and Slaving* (1927).

It appears from a calculation printed in Williams' work on the Liverpool slave trade, that during the eleven years from 1783 to 1793, 878 slavers owned in Liverpool, imported to the West Indies, 303,737 slaves whose estimated value amounted to the total of £15,186,850—a brilliantly successful traffic that brought great wealth to the principal adventurers and an unhappy reputation to the busy port of Liverpool.

**Source G:** from a speech by Sir W. Young during the debate on the abolition of the Slave Trade, 1806.

The question is, not whether there be some evil attending the Slave Trade; but whether, by the measure now before your Lordships, we shall increase or diminish the amount of human misery in the world . . . If you could improve the whole Continent of Africa by this vote, it would be a good measure indeed, but that is out of the question. One half of it is made up of slaves. Then what will be gained to the cause of humanity after you agree to abolish the Slave Trade, supposing you be able to abolish it? I believe that if you were able to carry the question of abolition today, not one less slave would be taken away from the coast of Africa. It has been said that America is about to give up the whole of the Slave Trade. My Lords, I believe that to be no more than a speculation. But suppose North America should give up this traffic. Do you think, My Lords, that South America will give it up? Do you think the Portuguese or the Spaniards will give it up? Certainly they will not. Every man who looks at the thing must plainly see that our giving up this is nothing more than resigning into the hands of the Portuguese and Spaniards that profit which, at present, is our own.

**Source H:** from Richard Lander, *Records of Captain Clapperton's Last Expedition to Africa* (1830).

As soon as a vessel arrives at her place of destination, the crew discharge her light cargo, with the manacles intended for the slaves, and land the captain at the same time. The vessel then cruises along the coast to take in cloth, ivory, a little gold dust, etc. If a British man-of-war be near, the crew, having nothing on board to excite suspicion, in most cases contrive to get their vessel searched while trading with the natives . . . They return to the place where their cargo had been loaded, and communicate with the captain on shore . . . who then takes the opportunity to tell his crew the exact time at which he will be ready to embark. The vessel then cruises a second time up and down the coast, till the appointed day approaches, when she proceeds to take in her living cargo.

[*END OF SOURCES FOR SPECIAL TOPIC 5*]

1998

## SPECIAL TOPIC 6: THE AMERICAN REVOLUTION

**Study the sources below and then answer the questions in the accompanying question paper.**

**Source A:** from an examination of Benjamin Franklin, 13 February 1766.

Q. What was the temper of America towards Great Britain before the year 1763?

A. The best in the world. They submitted willingly to the government of the Crown, and paid, in all their courts, obedience to acts of Parliament. Numerous as the people are in the several provinces, they cost you nothing in forts, citadels, garrisons or armies, to keep them in subjection. They were governed by this country at the expense only of a little pen, ink and paper. They had not only a respect, but an affection for Great Britain; for its laws, its customs and manners, and even a fondness for its fashions, that greatly increased the commerce. Natives of Britain were always treated with a particular regard. To be an Old England man was, of itself, a character of some respect, and gave a kind of rank among us.

Q. And what is their temper now?

A. O, very much altered.

Q. Did you ever hear the authority of Parliament to make laws for America questioned?

A. The authority of Parliament was allowed to be valid in all laws, except such as should lay internal taxes. It was never disputed in laying duties to regular commerce.

**Source B:** from a speech by Edmund Burke in Parliament, 22 March 1775.

First, the people of the colonies are descendants of Englishmen. England, Sir, is a nation which I hope still respects, and formerly adored, her freedom. The colonists emigrated from you, when this part of your character was most predominant. They took this bias and direction the moment they parted from your hands. They are therefore not only devoted to liberty, but to liberty according to English ideas, and on English principles . . . They took infinite pains to teach, as a fundamental principle, that, in all monarchies, the people must themselves possess the power of granting their own money, or no shadow of liberty could exist. The colonies draw from you, as with their life-blood, these ideas and principles. Their love of liberty, as with you, fixed and attached on this specific point of taxing. Liberty might be safe, or might be endangered in twenty other ways, without their being much pleased or alarmed. Here they felt its pulse; and as they found that beat, they thought themselves sick or sound.

**Source C:** from J. R. Pole, *Foundations of American Independence* (1972).

For years American spokesmen had been arguing that the constitution gave them all the protection which loyal subjects needed. In the process, the Americans had been forced to reconsider their own relationship to Britain under the constitution. However the mere existence of a Continental Congress implied that if redress of these grievances were not obtainable when all the colonies spoke together, then redress would have to be sought by other means. The idea that the Congress might see its duty as submission contradicted recent American experience. British obstinacy narrowed American choices, but many colonists still hoped for a reprieve.

**Source D:** from a speech by Patrick Henry to the Continental Congress, 1774.

Government is dissolved. Fleets and armies and the present state of things show that Government is dissolved. Where are your land marks, your boundaries of colonies? We are in a state of nature, Sir . . . The distinctions between Virginians, Pennsylvanians, New Yorkers and new Englanders are no more. I am not a Virginian, but an American.

**Source E:** from a letter by Edmund Burke to a friend, May 1775.

All our prospects of American reconciliation are, I fear, over. A detail of men was sent to destroy a magazine which the Americans were forming at a village called Concord. It proceeded with secrecy and speed. But the Americans were alert and conveyed their stores, all but four pieces of cannon and some flour, to a more distant town called Worcester. The people rose, without order or officers, and fell upon the troops on their return. Lord Percy was sent out to support the first party, which without his assistance would most certainly never have returned. He too would have been defeated, had it not been for two pieces of artillery which he had the precaution to take. The troops behaved well, and retreated thirteen miles in pretty good order. Their loss did not exceed 70 killed, and probably about the same number wounded. The Provincials harassed them the whole way. Their loss was thirty nine. During the time of this strange irregular engagement, expresses were sent to every part of America with astonishing rapidity, and the whole Northern part of the Continent was immediately under arms.

**Source F:** from a letter by Joseph Warren to Samuel Adams, May 1775.

I see more and more the necessity of establishing a civil government here, and such a government as shall be sufficient to control the military forces, not only of this colony, but also such as shall be sent to us from the other colonies. The continent must strengthen and support with all its weight the civil authority here. Otherwise our soldiery will lose the ideas of right and wrong, and will plunder, instead of protecting, the inhabitants. This is but too evident already. I assure you that, unless some authority sufficient to restrain the irregularities of this army is established, we shall very soon find ourselves involved in greater difficulties than you can imagine.

**Source G:** from Lawrence S. Kaplan, *The American Revolution and a Candid World* (1977).

France's decision for alliance was a decision for war with Britain, and it confirmed American independence, if not victory on the battlefield. Given the turmoil of the Congress, the divisions within the new nation, and the uncertainties of the military results, France gave the United States a remarkable gift—that of a successful conclusion to the Revolution. It agreed to renounce its concerns with former colonies in the New World, and to maintain "the liberty, sovereignty and independence absolute and unlimited of the said United States, as well in matters of government as in commerce". In the short run the benefits outweighed any debits.

**Source H:** from the *Blackwell Encyclopedia of the American Revolution* (1991).

Until peace was concluded in 1783, Quebec remained securely in British hands. The colony had, during the American revolution, come to possess a distinctive constitutional and legal structure which French Canadians began to view as theirs by right: a bulwark to their own separate identity within North America and the British Empire.

More than 35,000 loyalists eventually made their way in the early 1780s to Nova Scotia and more than 10,000 to Quebec. Their arrival compelled the British authorities to create three new colonies in British North America: Upper Canada, which is present day Ontario, New Brunswick and Cape Breton Island. The loyalists obviously strengthened the pro-British and anti-American bias of what remained of British North America, for they, like most Nova Scotians and residents of Quebec, had rejected the American revolution and a great deal that it represented.

[*END OF SOURCES FOR SPECIAL TOPIC 6*]

1998

## SPECIAL TOPIC 7: THE ENLIGHTENMENT IN SCOTLAND

**Study the sources below and then answer the questions in the accompanying question paper.**

**Source A:** An Edinburgh Playbill of 1756.

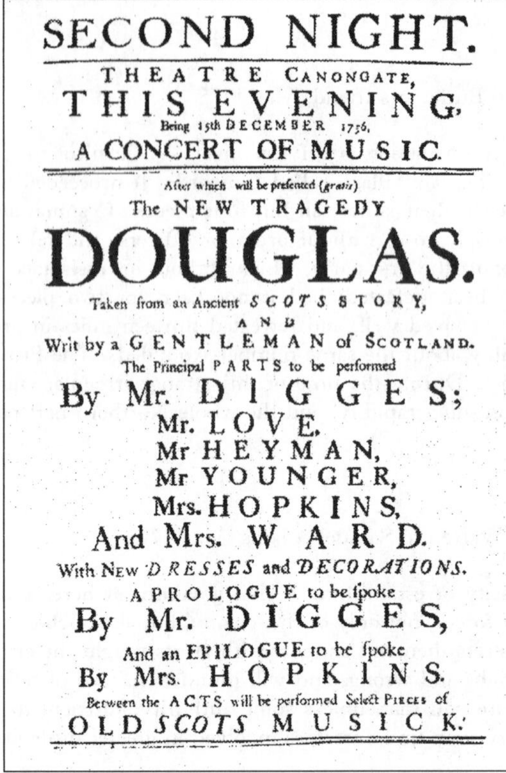
SECOND NIGHT.
THEATRE CANONGATE,
THIS EVENING
Being 15th DECEMBER 1756,
A CONCERT OF MUSIC.
After which will be presented (gratis)
The NEW TRAGEDY
DOUGLAS.
Taken from an Ancient SCOTS STORY,
AND
Writ by a GENTLEMAN of SCOTLAND.
The Principal PARTS to be performed
By Mr. DIGGES;
Mr. LOVE,
Mr HEYMAN,
Mr YOUNGER,
Mrs. HOPKINS,
And Mrs. WARD.
With NEW DRESSES and DECORATIONS.
A PROLOGUE to be spoke
By Mr. DIGGES,
And an EPILOGUE to be spoke
By Mrs. HOPKINS.
Between the ACTS will be performed Select PIECES of
OLD SCOTS MUSICK.

**Source B:** from Rev. Alexander Carlyle, "A Comparison of two Eminent Characters" in J. Kinley (ed.) *Anecdotes and Characters of the Times* (1973).

It was peculiar to this city and to this period, that one could arrive from the country in the afternoon, and be almost certain of assembling such men as David Hume and Adam Smith, and Blair and Robertson and John Home and Adam Ferguson in a tavern by 7 o'clock, which was the hour of supper in those days and the chief time of convivial entertainment, till about the year 1760. Those circumstances contributed not a little to that harmony which then reigned among an order of men, said proverbially to be of irritable minds.

**Source C:** from the preface to William Robertson, *History of Scotland* (1759).

As the same passions which inflamed parties in that age have descended to their posterity; as almost every event in Mary's reign has become the object of doubt or dispute; the eager spirit of controversy soon discovered that without some evidence more authentic and more impartial than that of such historians, none of the points in question could be decided with certainty. Records have therefore been searched, original papers produced, and public archives, as well as the collections of private men, have been ransacked by the zeal and curiosity of writers of different parties.

No History of Scotland that merits any attention has appeared since these Collections were published. By consulting them, I have been enabled, in many instances, to correct the inaccuracies of former historians, to avoid their mistakes and to detect their misinterpretations.

But many important papers have escaped the notice of these industrious collectors; and, after all they have produced to light, much still remained in darkness, unobserved or published. It was my duty to search for these, and I found this unpleasant task attended with considerable value.

**Source D:** from Adam Smith, *The Wealth of Nations* (1776).

In the present state of the Scotch Universities, I do most sincerely look upon them as, in spite of all their faults, without exception the best seminaries of learning that are to be found anywhere in Europe.

**Source E:** from Bruce Lenman, *Integration, Enlightenment and Industrialisation* (1992).

This rock-like stability in both the social and the political structure of an increasingly prosperous land was the essential precondition for the continued flowering of Scottish intellectual and artistic life, and this for two reasons. Firstly, prosperity generated the revenues required for the enlightened patronage of the arts and learning. Secondly, the governing classes were not tempted by fear of social upheaval, into a blind opposition to any form of critical thought.

**Source F:** a list of literature published by Scottish Ministers 1759–1792, excluding all religious works and sermons.

| | | |
|---|---|---|
| 1759 | William Robertson | *History of Scotland* |
| 1761 | Matthew Stewart | *Tracts, Physical & Mathematical* |
| 1762 | George Campbell | *Dissertation on Miracles* |
| 1762–1770 | Adam Dickson | *Treatise on Agriculture* |
| 1764 | Thomas Reid | *Inquiry into the Human Mind* |
| 1767 | Adam Ferguson | *Essay on Civil Society* |
| 1769 | Adam Ferguson | *Institutes of Moral Philosophy* |
| 1769 | John Home | *The Fatal Discovery* |
| 1769 | William Wilkie | *Moral Fables in Verse* |
| 1771–1785 | Robert Henry | *History of Great Britain* |
| 1774 | Alexander Gerard | *Essay on Genius* |
| 1777 | William Robertson | *History of America* |
| 1783 | Hugh Blair | *Lectures on Rhetoric* |
| 1785 | Thomas Reid | *Essays on Intellectual Powers* |
| 1788 | Adam Dickson | *Husbandry of the Ancients* |
| 1788 | John Playfair | *Barometrical Measurements* |
| 1788 | John Walker | *Motion of Sap in Trees* |
| 1790 | John Playfair | *Astronomy of the Brahmins* |
| 1792 | John Walker | *Institutes of Natural History* |

**Source G:** from Thomas Pennant, *A Tour in Scotland 1769* (1771).

The clergy of Scotland, the most decent and consistent in their conduct of any set of men I ever met with of their order, are at present much changed from the furious, illiterate and enthusiastic teachers of the old times. They have taken up the mild method of persuasion, instead of the cruel discipline of punishment. Science almost universally flourishes among them, their discourse is improving and the table they entertain the stranger at is decent and hospitable.

**Source H:** from Bruce Lenman, *Integration, Enlightenment and Industrialisation* (1992).

Henry Mackenzie was a central figure in Edinburgh intellectual life to the end of his days, which came the year before the demise of his close friend Walter Scott. In a periodical called *The Lounger* in December 1786 Mackenzie wrote the first important review of Burns, praising his "unimitable delicacy" and "rapt and inspired melancholy". Though the *literati*, including Hugh Blair, the Reverend Professor of Rhetoric, and Dugald Stewart, the philosopher, responded enthusiastically to the very misleading image of Burns as "the unlettered ploughman" (which he was not despite his own and Mackenzie's publicity on this theme) they were hostile to the Scots tongue. They would have turned Burns into a sentimental spouter of neo-classical English. James Beattie produced in 1787, when Burns was in Edinburgh, a list of Scotticisms to be avoided.

[*END OF SOURCES FOR SPECIAL TOPIC* 7]

## SPECIAL TOPIC 8: PATTERNS OF MIGRATION: SCOTLAND 1830s–1930s

**Study the sources below and then answer the questions in the accompanying question paper.**

**Source A:** from a report, *Glasgow Herald*, 16 December 1861.

It is now eleven o'clock and the public houses and singing saloons are pouring forth their tenants at will, and noisy, troublesome tenants assuredly they are . . . As we looked at a convenient distance an excited navvy came staggering down the street, swearing by all the saints in the Irish calendar "that never a boy in Donegal was the man to give him a beating". If such was really the case in Donegal, he had not long to wait in the Saltmarket for a "turn up"; for elbowing his way through the crowd and yelling like a hyena, a gigantic collier leaped in front of the luckless navvy and knocked him into the gutter without apology . . . The shebeens up and down the dark lanes are now opening up, the cold is also taking effect, and gradually the crowd melts away, some in the direction of these drinking dens, while others seek the shelter of their miserable homes.

**Source B:** J.E. Handley, *The Irish in Scotland*, (1970).

Much of the racial bitterness in Scotland against the Irish found physical expression in the pugnacity excited by heavy drinking at the weekend. In those drunken brawls commentators were apt to discover in an overwhelming degree the malignant influence of the Irish immigrant. These scenes of drunkenness and brutality might be witnessed almost every Sunday morning in the working-class districts of Edinburgh.

Drink made [the Irishman] quarrelsome and argument slid easily from the muscles in his tongue to the muscles in his arms. Living in an atmosphere of religious and political differences he required only the trigger touch of liquor to explode into physical violence. Weapons were freely used in those fights. Shunned as they often were by their Scottish neighbours, the immigrants stood shoulder to shoulder when rows occurred, and one man's quarrel often invoked the practical sympathy of the whole Irish neighbourhood. When the police interfered they rallied to rescue the prisoners from their hands. Violent riots occasionally among the colliers and iron-workers of Scottish and Irish nationalities kept the inhabitants of mining towns in a state of terror for days. This racial prejudice was particularly bitter in the early days of immigration.

**Source C:** from R. Swift, *The Irish in Britain 1815–1914* (1990).

A variety of factors needs to be considered in any attempt to explain the over-representation of the Irish in certain categories of criminal behaviour . . . It was in fact the poorest Irish who were associated in the public mind with crime and disorder . . . Moreover, much Irish criminality was clearly the by-product of a poverty-ridden and brutalising slum environment . . . There is also the charge that the over-representation of the Irish in the statistics of crime was the result of anti-Irish prejudice. This may have been so, but it is important to recognise that the stereotype of the brutalised Irish "Paddy" was well entrenched in the public mind even before the large scale immigration of the 1840s and 1850s . . . It also, of course, influenced the attitudes of the police and magistrates in their attempts to combat crime and disorder. Indeed, the over-representation of the Irish in the statistics of crime has to be seen, in part, in the context of the growth and development of local policing during the period. The essential targets of the "New Police" forces which emerged from 1829 onwards were varieties of street crime—drunkenness, disorderly behaviour, petty theft—in short, the very offences for which the Irish had acquired a legendary reputation.

**Source D:** from the twelfth report on Scottish prisons, quoted in the *Glasgow Herald*, 10 September 1847.

In travelling the country on my inspection tours I found that there had been a general fear of an increase in crime owing to the presence in different parts of large numbers of men employed in making railroads; but the result has shown that there was little foundation for this fear. The whole number of railway labourers committed to prison had been but small, and with few exceptions . . . the offences have been of a minor description, chiefly drunken quarrels. If superior arrangements had been made for the comfort of the railway labourers and for keeping them out of temptation . . . there would no doubt have been still fewer offences . . . in Roxburghshire, where I was informed there had, on average, been 1,500 men employed on the railway for some months, the average number of prisoners of this class, at any one time, had been only two. Mr Vere, the resident sheriff at Lanark, said that he was astonished at the general good conduct of the railway labourers and that, in proportion to their numbers, he thought there were fewer offences committed by the railway labourers than at most of the iron works in the district.

**Source E:** from the evidence of the Rev. William Gordon, resident priest of Greenock and Port Glasgow, *Report on the Irish Poor in Great Britain* (1836).

The Irish in this town are treated with a kind of exclusive policy, principally by the lower classes . . . The religious prejudice may probably also contribute something; this is now fast wearing away . . . There is a kind of advance to assimilation of feeling with the Scotch in the children of the Irish born in this country, which I attribute mainly to their education . . . We now have a school of our own, where we educate children of our congregation; the attendance is about 120 a day. Many of them, on account of the poverty of their parents, are forced to work during the day, and for these there is an evening school.

**Source F:** C. Whatley, *The Industrial Revolution in Scotland* (1997).

Prepared to accept lower wages, the Irish tended to be drawn into easier-to-enter trades such as handloom weaving, where they accounted for around 30 per cent of the workforce by the later 1830s. They were utilised by employers who exploited the opportunities their presence provided to introduce "blackleg" labour into coal mines for example, or to do the burdensome jobs such as ironstone mining, along with certain unskilled work where they were more numerous than the Scots. Resentment on the part of those sections of the native population who felt the direct effects of low-wage competition, and the fact that the religion of the majority of migrants was Roman Catholicism, heightened social tensions in mining and weaving towns and villages in Presbyterian counties such as Lanarkshire and Ayrshire. These tensions were increased when Irish Protestants (at least 25 per cent of the immigrant stream) brought with them a militant Orangeism.

[*END OF SOURCES FOR SPECIAL TOPIC 8*]

1998

## SPECIAL TOPIC 9: THE THIRD FRENCH REPUBLIC 1871–1914

**Study the sources below and then answer the questions in the accompanying question paper.**

**Source A:** drawing, "Le Traitre", from *Le Petit Journal*, 13 January 1895.

LE TRAITRE

**Source B:** from the secret diary of M. Paléologue, French Foreign Office official, 2 July 1898.

Delcassé wanted to question me about the Dreyfus case. By way of introduction he said:

"Talk to me with complete frankness; I shall be equally frank with you. We shall have to work together a great deal; I know you are worthy of all my confidence, so grant me yours."

I described to him how I had come to believe the 1894 trial was a put-up job, organised by subordinates to cover those really guilty of treason. I added that most of the documents used to incriminate Dreyfus seemed to me to be highly suspect. Delcassé sat still and silent while I talked, and when I had finished he said:

"You mentioned 'those really guilty'. So there are several?"

"That is what I think."

"I do not ask whom you suspect, because you have mentioned no names."

"I have mentioned no names because there is still too much uncertainty and conjecture about my suspicions."

"I approve your attitude. But I want to know your view of the role of General Boisdeffre and General Gonse."

"They are dupes in the matter."

"But Boisdeffre is very intelligent."

"Boisdeffre, yes. But he is easy-going, dislikes trouble and is terribly afraid of abuse in the nationalist Press. The slightest attack, the slightest criticism, by Rochefort or Drumont throws him into a panic."

**Source C:** from L. Blum, *Souvenirs sur L'Affaire* (1935).

The Dreyfusards have been accused of engineering a treacherous plot to divide France and tear it apart. But they did not and I think could not have suspected that there would be a Dreyfus Affair. For them everything was clear, luminous, obvious, and they did not doubt that universal reason must be persuaded by this truth. For the moment, at the end of the holidays [of 1897] public opinion was calm and indifferent; it was unaware and expected nothing. Yet when the truth was revealed what a generous cry would be heard throughout France! The nation had abhorred the crime as one, and as one it would proclaim the error and set it right! Three years before, people had wondered what punishments could chastise the traitor enough; now they would wonder what praises and rewards would even begin to rehabilitate the victim.

**Source D:** from K. Randell, *France: The Third Republic 1870–1914* (1986).

Politically conscious France had been divided into two camps, the Dreyfusards and the anti-Dreyfusards, for there were very few people of any education or social standing who were able to remain neutral. Often according to previous prejudice or general disposition, each person felt obliged to be either for Dreyfus or against him. Those who were anti-Semites, fervent nationalists, in favour of a militarily strong France, believers in discipline and authority, hostile to a parliamentary democracy or supporters of the Catholic Church tended to be against Dreyfus. Those who were active Republicans, socialists, pacifists or anti-clericals tended to be in favour of him. It is said, although without any quantitative evidence being presented, that the Affair . . . divided families, ended long-established friendships and even destroyed business partnerships such was the violence of the emotion it generated. For two years the Affair was the main headline news story, and politics seemed to be concerned with little else.

**Source E:** a poem by E. Pouget, an anarchist, written *c.* 1889.

The Republic she promised, but she lied,
she just pushes the little man aside,
with the powerful she plays,
with the tyrants she lays,
while in the streets our brothers have died.

**Source F:** from J.F. McMillan, *Twentieth Century France: Politics and Society 1898–1991* (1992).

Industrial workers worked long hours—at least 10, sometimes as many as 14, more usually 11. By 1914 one of the most important trade-union demands was for the eight-hour day and a shorter working week. Factory workers were also preoccupied with improving conditions at their places of work. The introduction of machinery on a large scale increased the risks of industrial injuries. Wages, as always, were a sensitive issue. It is true that they increased steadily after 1890, perhaps by as much as 30–60 per cent. Adjusted for rises in the cost of living, "real" wages were still rising, at least until about 1909. Diet improved, as workers spent a lower percentage of their earnings on food and at the same time ate a little more meat, vegetables and fruit. But the economic conditions of working-class life remained precarious. Wages were still too low to allow for any saving, or planning for the future.

**Source G:** from J.P.T. Bury, *France 1840–1940* (1969 edition).

The social problem had once again come to the fore during the years following the Dreyfus Affair. Under Millerand's guidance at the Ministry of Commerce some important measures had been taken to deal with labour problems. A Direction du Travail or Labour Department had been set up under the presidency of Arthur Fontaine, one of the most remarkable of the civil servants of the régime. A Conseil Supérieur du Travail had been established on which Trade Unions were given representation and much encouragement was given to Union organization. Furthermore, in 1900 the Waldeck-Rousseau Cabinet had secured the passage of a law for the gradual reduction to ten hours of the working day.

**Source H:** from R. de Jouvenel, *La République des Camarades* (1914).

This country no longer has institutions. However, it gets along admirably without them. France is a fortunate country, where the soil is generous, the craftsmen ingenious, wealth is divided up. Here, politics is according to individual taste; it is not the be-all and end-all of people's lives.

And this country lets itself be gently run by men who have no pretensions to provide it with arrogant doctrine, a superior government, certain justice or brutal truth. It does not seek to borrow its prosperity from its institutions; it simply prospers.

[*END OF SOURCES FOR SPECIAL TOPIC 9*]

1998

**SPECIAL TOPIC 10: AFRICAN SOCIETIES AND EUROPEAN IMPERIALISM 1880–1914**

**Study the sources below and then answer the questions in the accompanying question paper.**

**Source A:** from the Convention of Pretoria, 3 August 1881.

Her Majesty's Commissioners for the settlement of the Transvaal territory . . . do hereby undertake and guarantee . . . that from the 8th day of August 1881, complete self-government . . . will be accorded to the Transvaal territory . . .

Her Majesty reserves to herself, her heirs and successors, the right to appoint a British Resident in the said State; the right to move troops through the said State in time of war . . .; and the control of the external relations of the said State, including the conclusion of treaties . . .

**Source B:** from the Convention of Pretoria, 3 August 1881.

The following will be the duties and functions of the British Resident:

In regard to Natives within the Transvaal State he will . . . report to the Transvaal authorities any cases of ill-treatment of Natives, or attempts to incite Natives to rebellion . . .; use his influence with the Natives in favour of law and order; and . . . take such steps for the protection of the persons and property of Natives as are consistent with the laws of the land.

**Source C:** a French caricature on the Jameson Raid, 29 December 1895. The figure with the monocle represents Joseph Chamberlain, the smaller figure Dr Jameson.

**Source D:** from a poem by the Poet Laureate, C. Austin, on the Jameson Raid, 1895.

Wrong! Is it wrong? Well, may be;
  But I'm going just the same,
Do they think me a Burgher's baby,
  To be scared by a scolding name?
They may argue and prate and order;
  Go tell them to save their breath;
Then, over the Transvaal border,
  And gallop for life or death!

Let lawyers and statesmen addle
  Their heads over points of law;
If sound be our sword, and saddle,
  And gun-gear, who cares a straw?
When men of our own blood pray us
  To ride to their kinsfolk's aid,
Not heaven itself shall stay us,
  From the rescue they call a raid.

**Source E:** from a report of a speech by Sir William Harcourt, *The Times*, 15 June 1901.

With reference to this war I regard it as the greatest disaster which in modern times has befallen the British nation, both in its conduct and in what I fear must be its consequences . . .

In what condition do we now stand? That is just what we are not told . . . Ten months ago we were told that the war was over. Ever since then we have been treated to . . . detachments of the same kind of representation, and every announcement is followed by a fresh breaking out of the flames, and we are expecting every morning in some telegram to rejoice that we are slowly devastating a country which is our own; that we are killing and wounding a people we have recently made our own subjects. We are told, "Oh! it will soon be over and the Boers will settle down; it will be all right". Yes, we are told that by people who said the thing would be over in a few weeks at a cost of ten millions and by the assistance of 20,000 men.

**Source F:** from the *Liberia Bulletin*, number 14 (1899).

It is given to few men to think clearly on the Africa question. One of these few men is Sir George Goldie. He has said that Africa should be divided up into that region which white men can colonize in the true sense of the word—a region so admirably represented by South Africa; then a region which white men can colonize to much the same extent as they can in India—the highlands of British Central Africa; and then that region which white men cannot colonize at all in the true sense of the word—West Africa. This is politically the Africa we must keep in our mind, remembering England wants markets as well as colonies. And so West Africa, the richest raw material market in the world, is as much use to her as a colony would be.

**Source G:** from R. Robinson and J. Gallagher with A. Denny, *Africa and the Victorians* (1974 edition).

To judge by their actions before 1895, British ministers felt no urgent need to develop West Africa. They did not act like men desperately putting imperial power and capital to work in West Africa for the purpose of raising new markets and sources of supply. They were slow to bring the existing field of commerce under imperial rule. They were even slower to use administration in West Africa directly to graft new forms of production into the native economy. To imagine that the needs of British industry drove the late-Victorians to acquire enlarged tropical estates in West Africa, is to exaggerate their activity and misread their minds.

It is often supposed that tropical Africa was brought under imperial rule to create more business for Britain. But in West Africa, before 1895, it would be truer to say that the merchant was expected to create empire, that government . . . expected him to do without imperial rule, to make do with the protection of a sphere of influence, and to pioneer his own way inland.

[*END OF SOURCES FOR SPECIAL TOPIC 10*]

1998

## SPECIAL TOPIC 11: APPEASEMENT AND THE ROAD TO WAR, TO 1939

**Study the sources below and then answer the questions in the accompanying question paper.**

**Source A:** from the editorial, *Aberdeen Press and Journal*, 9 March 1936.

### WATCH ON THE RHINE

Once again, Herr Hitler has broken up a treaty, and followed up the breach by offering to negotiate a new one. In defiance of the Treaty of Versailles and the Locarno Pact, he, on Saturday, sent troops to occupy the demilitarised zone on both banks of the Rhine. A few hours later, in a Reichstag speech, he proposed a new treaty between Germany, France and Belgium, with Britain and Italy as guarantors . . .

In this country, few people will be disposed to quarrel with Herr Hitler for breaking the Versailles Treaty. It is generally recognised to have been impracticable because it was too harsh. Many parts of the treaty are now acknowledged to have been mistaken . . . but the breach of the Locarno Pact is a different matter . . . Germany has torn it up on an utterly flimsy pretext.

**Source B:** from R. Henig, *The Origins of the Second World War* (1985).

Why were the British and French governments not prepared to take stronger action against Hitler in 1936, when he had demonstrated so clearly his intention to destroy the Versailles settlement by force, if necessary? . . . The British government had been unhappy about the Versailles settlement from the start, believing it to be harsh and in some respects unjust. British governments and the British public therefore sympathised to a considerable extent with Hitler's determination to shake off the shackles of Versailles and establish Germany once again as a leading European power. In both Britain and France, the memory of the First World War remained strong. Successive governments were determined to do all they could to avoid being dragged into such a conflict again, and their electorates strongly supported policies geared to defence and to deterrence. In Britain, considerable disarmament had taken place . . . partly because of the widespread support for programmes of arms limitation which it was hoped would preserve peace.

**Source C:** cartoon by David Low, *Evening Standard*, 13 January 1937.

NON-INTERVENTION POKER

[1]Tony = Anthony Eden

**Source D:** from a letter sent from Spain by Jack Jones to the Labour Party, 9 July 1938.

We believe that there can be no compromise between Fascism and Democratic ideals, for which we ourselves have come here to fight. We feel ourselves wholly at one with the determination of the Spanish people to drive out the invaders of their country. As members of the Labour Party, we urge our leaders to turn a deaf ear to talk of compromise, and continue to press ever more vigorously the Party's declared policy; namely, the demand that the British Government's support of "non-intervention" be reversed, and that the right be restored to the Spanish Republic freely to purchase arms.

Nothing could be more encouraging to the work of those of us fighting with the British Battalion than to feel that we are being supported by the vigorous efforts of all the Democratic forces of Britain led by the Labour Party. In that struggle, we are proud to act in the advance guard, and pledge ourselves to do all in our power to maintain the high reputation already gained by the Battalion in Spain.

**Source E:** from a speech by Clement Attlee, MP, leader of the Labour Party, in the House of Commons, October 1938.

There was a conflict in the mind of every thoughtful person in the country when he heard that this settlement had been arrived at. On the one hand, there was enormous relief that war had been averted for the time being; on the other, there was a sense of humiliation and foreboding for the future . . .

The events of the last few days constitute one of the greatest diplomatic defeats that this country and France have ever sustained . . . It is a tremendous victory for Herr Hitler. Without firing a shot, by the mere display of military force, he has achieved a dominating position in Europe which Germany failed to win after four years of war. . . He has destroyed the last fortress of democracy in Eastern Europe which stood in the way of his ambitions.

**Source F:** from an editorial, *Aberdeen Press and Journal*, 3 October 1938.

In this country, and in many others as well, yesterday was a day of thanksgiving for the avoidance of war. Of the utter thankfulness that is felt there is no question. No one who lived through the 1914–1918 struggle, whether facing imminent death in the trenches or in the nerve-wracked atmosphere at home, could contemplate another war of the same proportions without the deepest abhorrence . . . Those who, even yet, are critical of the terms of the settlement, cannot but join in the universal relief. And the determination of Mr Chamberlain in bringing it about is abundantly recognised. He received great aid, certainly, from the French Premier, the Duce and the American President—it would be wrong, and ungrateful, not to recognise the part they played. But the dissipation of the war cloud is above all the work of the British Prime Minister. For lives of suffering spared, for horrors averted, Europe's thanks are due to him.

[*END OF SOURCES FOR SPECIAL TOPIC 11*]

## SPECIAL TOPIC 12: THE ORIGINS AND DEVELOPMENT OF THE COLD WAR 1945–1985

**Study the sources below and then answer the questions in the accompanying question paper.**

**Source A:** from Nikita Khrushchev, *Khrushchev Remembers* (1970).

Our potential enemy—our principal, our most powerful, our most dangerous enemy—was so far away from us that we couldn't have reached him with our air force. Only by building up a nuclear missile force could we keep the enemy from unleashing war against us. As life has already confirmed, if we had given the West a chance, war would have been declared while Dulles was alive. But we were the first to launch rockets into space; we exploded the most powerful nuclear device; we accomplished those feats first, ahead of the United States, England and France. Our accomplishments and our obvious might had a sobering effect on the aggressive forces in the United States, England, France and, of course, inside the Bonn [West German] government. They knew that they had lost the chance to strike at us without being punished.

**Source B:** from J.W. Mason, *The Cold War* (1996).

The half-decade from 1957 to 1962 has been called the "nuclear epoch", a time when the danger of nuclear war was greater than ever before or since. On 4 October 1957 the Soviet Union launched the first man-made satellite, called Sputnik, into orbit around the earth. It was a spectacular scientific achievement that alarmed the United States, not least because of its military implications. If the Soviets had a rocket capable of putting a satellite into orbit they could also produce a rocket with sufficient thrust to launch an inter-continental ballistic missile (ICBM) with a nuclear warhead against a target in the United States. At a stroke the Soviet Union seemed to have changed the East-West strategic balance.

. . . In fact, the so-called "missile gap" in favour of the Soviet Union turned out to be a myth. In 1960 the Soviet Union had a total of only 4 ICBMs and 145 long-range bombers. The United States had overwhelming nuclear strategic superiority throughout the 1950s.

**Source C:** from a speech by President John F. Kennedy, April 1961.

Should it ever appear that the American doctrine of non-interference merely conceals or excuses a policy of inaction—if the nations of this hemisphere should fail to meet their commitments against outside Communist penetration—then I want it clearly understood that this Government will not hesitate in meeting its primary obligations which are to the security of our Nation!

. . . It is clear that this Nation, in concert with all the free nations in this hemisphere, must take an ever closer and more realistic look at the menace of external Communist intervention and domination in Cuba. The American people are not complacent about Iron Curtain tanks and planes less than 90 miles from their shore. But a nation of Cuba's size is less a threat to our survival than it is a base for subverting the survival of other free nations throughout the hemisphere. It is not primarily our interest but theirs which is now, today, in the greater peril. It is for their sake as well as our own that we must show our will.

**Source D:** cartoon by Norman Mansbridge, *Punch*, 17 October 1962.

OVER THE GARDEN WALL

**Source E:** from a letter, from five Communist and Worker Parties in member countries of the Warsaw Pact, to the Central Committee of the Communist Party of Czechoslovakia, 15 July 1968.

> Our countries are linked to one another by treaties and agreements. These important mutual obligations . . . are based on the common aspiration to defend socialism and ensure the collective security of the socialist countries. Historic responsibility rests with our parties and peoples for ensuring that the revolutionary gains are not lost.
>
> Each of our parties is responsible not only to its own working class and its people, but also to the international working class and the world communist movement, and it cannot escape the obligations ensuing from this. We must therefore . . . be united in defending the gains of socialism, our security and the international position of the whole of the socialist community. That is why we believe that it is not only your task, but also ours, to administer a decisive rebuff to the anti-communist forces and to make decisive efforts to preserve the socialist system in Czechoslovakia.

**Source F:** from the editorial, *The Scotsman*, 22 August 1968.

Stalin imposed his cruel rigid brand of Communism on a dozen unwilling nations. Khrushchev invaded Hungary in 1956 to keep it imprisoned inside the Soviet Empire. Now the committee that presently rules Russia has shown that the basic principles are unchanged. Power must still be maintained by violence, never by popular consent . . .

The comparison between what happened yesterday and the invasion of Hungary in 1956 is inescapable. Mr Dubcek, unlike Mr Nagy, promised . . . and indeed tried, to maintain his country's loyalty to the Warsaw Pact . . .

Mr Dubcek recognised that the traditional, rigid, oppressive, orthodox Communism imposed on this country 20 years ago . . . and maintained without basic alteration until Mr Novotny was deposed earlier this year, was no longer tolerable, either spiritually or economically. He was mistaken, however, to hope that Russia had mellowed sufficiently to allow him to experiment with a new system. Nobody can tell, now, whether his attempt to reconcile Communism and freedom would have worked. The Soviet leaders feared . . . that freedom would, in the end, prevail over Communism. But they themselves have no suggestions to make; they offer instead the traditional remedy of repression.

**Source G:** from J. Steele, *World Power* (1983).

What can be calculated with some degree of certainty is the list of arguments for and against the invasion. The primary argument for the invasion was the Soviet fear that events in Czechoslovakia were drifting out of the party's control, and that Dubcek and his colleagues had shown neither the will nor the determination to control them. There was no prospect that the situation would improve. On the contrary, the longer they were allowed to develop, the less reversible the reforms would be. Sooner or later the reforms would give Czechoslovakia a form of ideological independence that would encourage the extremists to call for the country's departure from the Warsaw Pact, and the establishment of, at best, an alternative model of socialism, at worst, even a Western kind of social democracy, as had happened in Hungary in 1956.

. . . The second Soviet argument in favour of invasion was concern about the Prague Spring's effect on the rest of Eastern Europe, and even in the Soviet Union itself.

. . . Finally, there must have been a strong view in the Kremlin that Moscow could simply not afford another defection. In the last eight years they had lost Albania and China and seen Rumania become increasingly independent. To lose Czechoslovakia would be to risk the loss of the whole of Eastern Europe and the entire buffer zone they had managed to set up at the end of the war.

[*END OF SOURCES FOR SPECIAL TOPIC 12*]

1998

## SPECIAL TOPIC 13: IRELAND 1900–1985: A DIVIDED IDENTITY

**Study the sources below and then answer the questions in the accompanying question paper.**

**Source A:** from the *Belfast Telegraph*, 16 January 1913.

[The Southern Irish are] a band of men wholly unskilled in the arts of government and management of the businesses in which we are so vitally concerned . . . Ulster . . . will not exchange the stately rule and protection of the parliament of Great Britain for a bankrupt, intolerant and embittered assembly but little removed from the dignity and capacity of a parish council, and destitute of all justice and toleration.

**Source B:** an anonymous Irish ballad, 1914.

For hail or rain or frost or snow,
We're not going out to Flanders, O,
While there's fighting to be done at home.
Let your privates and commanders go.
Let Englishmen for England fight;
It's nearly time they started, O!

**Source C:** from C. Lawlor, *Britain and Ireland 1914–1923* (1983).

The outbreak of war in August 1914 had a consequence for Ireland as dramatic as its implications for the ultimate settlement of Europe. Before August 1914, the solution to the Irish question "belonged" to Asquith's Liberal government, but the combination of Ulster Unionists and Conservative opposition denied it to him. After that date, the importance of the Irish question became almost negligible by contrast with the gravity of the grand political and strategic issues arising out of the war. Before August 1914 Redmond's party of Irish MPs was prepared to recommend to their voters Asquith's schemes for home rule. Subsequently, the implications . . . of the war on Ireland changed the context of the demand in Ireland. Instead of home rule, the Irish wanted independence; instead of negotiation, they resorted to the use of force, both physical and moral. Asquith and Redmond, the names before the war, were replaced by Lloyd George and de Valera. Lloyd George was dependent on Conservative support, and de Valera on that of the gunmen.

**Source D:** a cartoon from 1918.

JOHN REDMOND: "Bad luck to their infernal machine with the foreign name. Every place it comes on the road I have lost any fares I had. I can't afford to give the poor beasts a feed of oats. I'm to blame myself. I'm a bit slow, and out of date."

**Source E:** from a journal written by an Irishwoman at the time of the Easter Rising, quoted in Magnus Magnusson, *Landlord or Tenant?* (1978).

Of course this is not Ireland's rebellion—only a Sinn Féin rising . . . How often have I laughed and quarrelled over the bare idea of an Irish Republic! It is so utterly un-Irish. Of course we want our country free from foreign rule. But anyone with sense can see that it must come by England's consent, not against England's will . . .

The Sinn Féin leaders were such good men. They died like saints . . . They have crushed us under a weight of sorrow and shame—but they meant the reverse. What wild madness came over them!

But, as sure as God's sun rises in the East, if England doesn't get things right—if there's not immediately conciliation, and love and mercy poured out on Ireland—all the Sinn Féin leaders will become heroes! . . . You know how Ireland is always merciful to the dead!

**Source F:** from the election manifesto of Sinn Féin, 1918.

Sinn Féin aims at securing the establishment of . . . [the Irish] Republic,

1 By withdrawing the Irish representation from the British parliament and by denying the right and opposing the will of the British government to legislate for Ireland.
2 By making use of any and every means to render impotent [powerless] the power of England to hold Ireland in subjection by military force or otherwise.
3 By the establishment of a [parliament] . . . as the supreme national authority to speak and act in the name of the Irish people.

Sinn Féin stands by the Proclamation of the Provisional Government of Easter 1916 . . . The present Irish members of the English parliament constitute an obstacle to be removed . . . By declaring their will to accept the status of a province instead of boldly taking their stand upon the right of the nation . . . [and] by their persistent endeavours to induce the young manhood of Ireland to don the uniform of our seven-century oppressor, and place their lives at the disposal of the military machine that holds our nation in bondage, they endeavour to barter away . . . the one great asset left to our nation.

**Source G:** from a Proclamation by Eamon de Valera, 14 December 1921.

TO THE IRISH PEOPLE

My friends

You have seen in the public Press the text of the proposed Treaty with Great Britain.

The terms of this agreement are in violent conflict with the wishes of the majority of this nation as expressed in the successive elections during the last three years.

I feel it my duty to inform you immediately that I cannot recommend the acceptance of this Treaty, either to Dail Eireann or the country. In this attitude I am supported by the Ministers of Home Affairs and Defence.

**Source H:** from "Notes by General Michael Collins", August 1922.

The Anti-Treaty party attempted to stampede meetings by revolver shootings, to wreck trains, the suppression of free speech, of the liberty of the Press, terrorisation and sabotage of a kind that we were familiar with a year ago. And with what object? With the sole object of preventing the people from expressing their will, and of making the government of Ireland by the representatives of the people as impossible as the English government was made impossible by the united forces a year ago.

Their policy had now become clear—to prevent the people's will being carried out because it differed from their own, to create trouble in order to break up the only possible national government, and to destroy the Treaty with utter recklessness as to the consequences.

[*END OF SOURCES FOR SPECIAL TOPIC 13*]

[*END OF SOURCES*]

SCOTTISH CERTIFICATE OF EDUCATION 1998

THURSDAY, 14 MAY
1.00 PM – 3.00 PM

# HISTORY
# HIGHER GRADE
## Paper II
## Questions

### SPECIAL TOPIC 1: NORMAN CONQUEST AND EXPANSION 1050–1153

**Answer *all* of the following questions.** *Marks*

1. How reliable is **Source A** as evidence of William's efforts to overcome opposition to his plans to invade England? 4

2. Why was there so much aristocratic emigration from Normandy between 1050 and 1153? 5

3. Explain why **Sources B** and **C** differ in their assessments of Odo of Bayeux. 5

4. How fully does **Source C** explain the reasons for the uprisings against William between 1066 and 1075? 6

5. Compare the views of Reynolds (**Source D**) and Brown (**Source E**) about the existence and development of feudalism in England. 5

6. Is there sufficient evidence in **Sources A**, **B**, **E** and **F** to argue that William introduced feudalism to England at the time of the Norman Conquest? 8

7. Does Bartlett (**Source G**) explain adequately why Norman knights colonised Scotland during the reign of David I? 5

8. To what extent was Scotland transformed by these Anglo-Norman settlers in the twelfth century? 7

**(45)**

[*END OF QUESTIONS ON SPECIAL TOPIC 1*]

## SPECIAL TOPIC 2: THE CRUSADES 1096–1204

**Answer *all* of the following questions.** *Marks*

**1.** Compare the views of Bartlett (**Source A**) and Riley-Smith (**Source B**) about the motives of crusaders. 4

**2.** In your opinion, which of these views is more accurate? Explain your answer. 6

**3.** How useful is **Source C** as evidence about the actions and attitudes of the crusaders during the First Crusade? 4

**4.** How fully do **Sources D** and **E** illustrate the role of the Italian towns during the Crusades? 5

**5.** What effect did the crusades have on trade patterns in the eastern Mediterranean between the eleventh and thirteenth centuries? Refer to **Source F** and your own knowledge. 6

**6.** How far are the views of Jones and Ereira (**Source G**) about Saladin supported by the evidence in **Source H**? 6

**7.** To what extent does **Source H** explain the failure of the Third Crusade? 6

**8.** Is there enough evidence in **Sources A**, **B**, **C** and **H** to argue that by 1200 the crusading ideal was in decline? 8

**(45)**

[*END OF QUESTIONS ON SPECIAL TOPIC 2*]

## SPECIAL TOPIC 3: TRADE AND TOWNS

**Answer *all* of the following questions.**

**1.** How typical of early medieval Scottish burghs was Perth (**Source A**)? 5

**2.** How reliable is King Alexander II's charter (**Source B**) as evidence for the existence of merchants' guilds in thirteenth-century Scottish burghs? 4

**3.** To what extent does King William I's charter (**Source C**) support the views of Lynch (**Source D**)? 5

**4.** To what extent did burghs control trade in Scotland? Refer to **Sources B**, **C**, **D** and **E** and your own knowledge. 8

**5.** How fully does **Source F** explain the functions and inter-relationships of local, regional and inter-regional trade? 7

**6.** Why was the area shown in **Source G** important for Scottish trade in the Middle Ages? 6

**7.** Explain the causes of the trends in the Scottish export trade shown in **Source H**. 5

**8.** What effects did these trends have on Scottish towns in the fifteenth century? 5

**(45)**

[*END OF QUESTIONS ON SPECIAL TOPIC 3*]

## SPECIAL TOPIC 4: SCOTLAND 1689–1715

**Answer *all* of the following questions.** *Marks*

1. How fully does **Source A** explain the growth of tension between Scotland and England in the period before the Union? 6

2. How far does the evidence in **Source B** support Fletcher's argument in **Source C**? 5

3. How useful is **Source D** as evidence of public feeling in Edinburgh during the Union debates? 4

4. How important was the issue described in **Source E** in the debates over Union? 6

5. To what extent were the arguments in **Source F** typical of those voiced by Scottish supporters of the Union? 6

6. How fully did the terms of the Treaty of Union meet the hopes expressed in **Source F**? 5

7. How important were the reasons given in **Sources C**, **E** and **F** in explaining why the Scottish Parliament accepted the Union? 8

8. How widespread at the time were the feelings expressed in **Source G**? 5

**(45)**

[*END OF QUESTIONS ON SPECIAL TOPIC 4*]

## SPECIAL TOPIC 5: THE ATLANTIC SLAVE TRADE

**Answer *all* of the following questions.**

1. How useful is **Source A** as evidence of conditions in the Middle Passage? 4

2. Compare the evidence in **Sources B** and **C** about the reactions of slaves to their enslavement. 5

3. How serious were the effects of the Slave Trade for African societies? 6

4. To what extent do **Sources D** and **E** reveal the methods used by abolitionists? 5

5. How far does **Source F** explain the importance of the Slave Trade to the British economy? 6

6. How well does the evidence in **Source H** support the arguments of Young in **Source G**? 5

7. How fully do **Sources E, F** and **G** illustrate the issues in the debate over the abolition of the Slave Trade? 8

8. What, in your opinion, was the main reason for the abolition of the British Slave Trade in 1807? 6

**(45)**

[*END OF QUESTIONS ON SPECIAL TOPIC 5*]

1998

## SPECIAL TOPIC 6: THE AMERICAN REVOLUTION

**Answer *all* of the following questions.** *Marks*

1. How useful is **Source A** as evidence of American attitudes towards British rule in the 1760s and early 1770s? 6

2. How important were government policies in changing relations between the British and Americans? 6

3. How fully does **Source B** illustrate the views of British sympathisers with the American cause? 6

4. How far does the evidence in **Source B** support the views of Pole in **Source C**? 5

5. Discuss the significance of **Source D** in the context of events at the time. 4

6. To what extent do you accept Burke's views (**Source E**) on the importance of the outbreak of fighting? 5

7. How fully do **Sources D**, **E**, **F** and **G** explain the British defeat in the American War of Independence? 8

8. To what extent does **Source H** explain changes in British policy towards Canada? 5

**(45)**

[*END OF QUESTIONS ON SPECIAL TOPIC 6*]

## SPECIAL TOPIC 7: THE ENLIGHTENMENT IN SCOTLAND

**Answer *all* of the following questions.**

1. How useful is **Source A** as evidence of changing attitudes towards the theatre in eighteenth-century Scotland? 4

2. How important a feature of the Scottish Enlightenment was the social life described in **Source B**? 5

3. How typical of writers of the period was Robertson's approach to history (**Source C**)? 5

4. Do you accept Adam Smith's views (**Source D**) on Scottish universities in the late eighteenth century? 6

5. To what extent does Lenman (**Source E**) explain the origins of the Scottish Enlightenment? 5

6. How great a contribution did the clergy make to the Scottish Enlightenment? Refer to **Sources F** and **G** and your own knowledge. 6

7. How fully do **Sources C**, **F** and **H** illustrate the cultural impact of the Enlightenment in Scotland? 8

8. To what extent did progressive attitudes affect the Scottish economy between 1750 and 1800? 6

**(45)**

[*END OF QUESTIONS ON SPECIAL TOPIC 7*]

## SPECIAL TOPIC 8: PATTERNS OF MIGRATION: SCOTLAND 1830s–1930s

**Answer *all* of the following questions.** *Marks*

1. Comment on the value of **Source A** as evidence about Irish immigrants to Scotland. 4

2. To what extent does the evidence in **Source A** support the views of Handley in **Source B**? 5

3. How far do you accept Swift's explanation (**Source C**) for the reputation of the immigrant Irish as criminals? 5

4. Assess the reliability of **Source D** as evidence of the conduct of Irish railway navvies. 4

5. How similar were the reasons for the movements of Irish and Highland migrants to Scottish cities between the 1830s and 1880s? 7

6. How accurately does **Source E** describe the part played by education in the lives of Irish immigrants to Scotland? 6

7. How fully do **Sources A**, **C** and **F** explain the existence of anti-Irish feelings in nineteenth-century Scotland? 8

8. How well did immigrant groups assimilate into Scottish society in the period from the 1830s to the 1930s? 6

**(45)**

[*END OF QUESTIONS ON SPECIAL TOPIC 8*]

## SPECIAL TOPIC 9: THE THIRD FRENCH REPUBLIC 1871–1914

**Answer *all* of the following questions.**

1. Explain the significance of the drawing (**Source A**) in the light of events at the time. 4

2. How reliable is **Source B** as evidence that Dreyfus was the victim of a conspiracy? 6

3. How accurately does Blum in **Source C** describe the expectations of the Dreyfusards in their campaign to free Dreyfus? 5

4. To what extent do **Sources A**, **B** and **C** support the judgements in **Source D** about the impact of the Dreyfus Affair on France? 8

5. How far does the evidence in **Source E** support McMillan's views in **Source F**? 5

6. How effectively did government action in the 1890s solve the problem of industrial unrest? Refer to **Source G** and your own knowledge. 6

7. How serious a threat to the survival of the Third Republic were the internal problems which it faced up to 1895? 7

8. How well does **Source H** describe the state of the Third Republic by 1914? 4

**(45)**

[*END OF QUESTIONS ON SPECIAL TOPIC 9*]

## SPECIAL TOPIC 10: AFRICAN SOCIETIES AND EUROPEAN IMPERIALISM 1880–1914

**Answer *all* of the following questions.** *Marks*

1. How successful was the Convention of Pretoria (**Source A**) in dealing with Anglo-Boer disputes? 6

2. Assess the value of **Source B** as evidence of British concern for the well-being of native Africans in the Transvaal. 4

3. Explain the significance of the cartoon (**Source C**) in the light of events at the time. 4

4. How fully do **Sources B, C** and **D** illustrate the deteriorating relations between Britain and the Transvaal in the 1880s and 1890s? 8

5. To what extent does **Source E** reflect British opinion at the time about the Boer War? 6

6. How well does the evidence in **Source F** support the views expressed in **Source G**? 5

7. How far did British policy towards West Africa, as illustrated in **Source G**, change after 1900? 6

8. Would you agree that colonial rivalry was a major cause of poor relationships between European Great Powers between 1880 and 1914? 6

**(45)**

[*END OF QUESTIONS ON SPECIAL TOPIC 10*]

## SPECIAL TOPIC 11: APPEASEMENT AND THE ROAD TO WAR, TO 1939

**Answer *all* of the following questions.**

1. How valuable is **Source A** as evidence about the issues raised by the German reoccupation of the Rhineland in March 1936? 4

2. ". . . Hitler's determination to shake off the shackles of Versailles . . ." (**Source B**). How accurate is this interpretation of German foreign policy between 1933 and 1936? 6

3. To what extent do you accept Henig's analysis (**Source B**) of the British and French response to the reoccupation of the Rhineland? 6

4. How well does **Source C** illustrate British policy towards the Spanish Civil War? 5

5. How typical of British opinion at the time were the views of Jack Jones in **Source D**? 5

6. Compare the views on the Munich crisis expressed in **Sources E** and **F**. 5

7. To what extent do you agree with Attlee's judgement (**Source E**) on the outcome of the Czech crisis? 6

8. How fully do **Sources A, B, C** and **F** explain the response of the British government to fascist aggression between 1936 and 1939? 8

**(45)**

[*END OF QUESTIONS ON SPECIAL TOPIC 11*]

## SPECIAL TOPIC 12: THE ORIGINS AND DEVELOPMENT OF THE COLD WAR 1945–1985

**Answer *all* of the following questions.** *Marks*

1. How useful is **Source A** in explaining Soviet policy towards the nuclear arms race during the 1950s? 4

2. To what extent do you accept Mason's views (**Source B**) on the development of the nuclear arms race? 6

3. "Our potential enemy . . ." (**Source A**). To what extent was rivalry between East and West a threat to world peace in the period 1945–1955? 6

4. How fully does President Kennedy in **Source C** explain the policy of the United States government towards Cuba? 6

5. Discuss the significance of **Source D** in the light of events at the time. 4

6. Compare the explanations given in **Sources E** and **F** for the Warsaw Pact invasion of Czechoslovakia in August 1968. 5

7. How accurate is *The Scotsman*'s analysis (**Source F**) of Soviet policy in Eastern Europe in the 1950s and 1960s? 6

8. How fully do **Sources A, C, F** and **G** illustrate the issues that caused tension between East and West between 1955 and 1970? 8

**(45)**

[*END OF QUESTIONS ON SPECIAL TOPIC 12*]

## SPECIAL TOPIC 13: IRELAND 1900–1985: A DIVIDED IDENTITY

**Answer *all* of the following questions.**

1. To what extent does **Source A** explain the reasons for Unionist opposition to Home Rule? 6

2. How valuable is **Source B** as evidence of Irish nationalist opinions towards participating in the First World War? 4

3. To what extent did political attitudes in Ireland change between 1914 and 1918? Refer to **Sources C**, **D** and **F** and your own knowledge. 8

4. How fully does **Source E** describe Irish reaction to the Easter Rising? 6

5. How serious a threat did **Source F** present to British authority in Ireland? 6

6. Compare the attitudes towards the Anglo-Irish Treaty expressed in **Sources G** and **H**. 5

7. What were the consequences of the statement by de Valera (**Source G**)? 5

8. Why was the creation of the Irish Free State followed by continued friction over the status of Ulster? 5

**(45)**

[*END OF QUESTIONS ON SPECIAL TOPIC 13*]

[*END OF QUESTION PAPER*]

SCOTTISH CERTIFICATE OF EDUCATION 1999

THURSDAY, 13 MAY
9.00 AM – 11.00 AM

# HISTORY
# HIGHER GRADE
## Paper I

### OPTION A: MEDIEVAL HISTORY

**Answer THREE questions selected from at least two Sections, one of which must be Section (a).**

#### Section (a): Medieval Society

1. To what extent was there a common manorial system throughout Scotland and England?
2. What was the most important contribution that monasteries made to medieval society?
3. "Life in twelfth-century towns and burghs was dominated by trading and manufacturing." Discuss.
4. How successful was Henry I in dealing with the problems which faced him as king of England?
5. Why did the argument between Henry II and Becket last for so long?

#### Section (b): Nation and King

6. Do you agree that King John of England was a very able monarch?
7. Was the destruction of the Angevin Empire the most important achievement of Philip II of France?
8. How great a contribution did William Wallace make to the Scottish victory in the Wars of Independence?
9. How important was the idea of the Community of the Realm among the barons in England, Scotland and France?

#### Section (c): Crisis of Authority

10. How successful were the English in the Hundred Years' War up to 1360?
11. How far was the Peasants' Revolt caused by a wish to abolish serfdom?
12. To what extent did the Avignon Papacy lead to a decline in the power and prestige of the Papacy in the fourteenth and fifteenth centuries?
13. Is it true that there was a crisis of political, religious and social authority in Europe in the fourteenth and fifteenth centuries?

## OPTION B: EARLY MODERN HISTORY

**Answer THREE questions selected from at least two Sections, one of which must be Section (a).**

### Section (a): Scotland and England in the Century of Revolutions (1603–1702)

1. How far can the political challenge to Charles I before 1629 be attributed to the policies of his father?

2. "It was the Scots who finally drove the King and the English Parliament to war." Do you agree?

3. Did the governments of 1649–1660 fail because they abandoned monarchy?

4. Was James II the main cause of the 1688–1689 revolution?

5. How far can religion be seen as the main challenge to royal authority in Britain between 1603 and 1702?

### Section (b): Royal Authority in 17th and 18th Century Europe

6. To what extent were Louis XIV's ministers responsible for the growth of his royal authority?

7. How seriously did financial problems limit Louis XIV's absolutism in action?

8. Why did Joseph II base his laws on the principles of the Enlightenment?

9. How far did Joseph II change the Austrian Empire?

### Section (c): The French Revolution: The Emergence of the Citizen State

10. How well did the Ancien Régime function?

11. Why did the challenge to French absolutism grow so much more serious during 1789?

12. How important was popular unrest in the destruction of the monarchy between 1790 and 1793?

13. Which government had the greatest impact on France between 1793 and 1799?

1999

## OPTION C: LATER MODERN HISTORY

**Answer THREE questions selected from at least two Sections, one of which must be Section (a).**

### Section (a): Britain 1850s–1979

1. How far had British governments abandoned the policy of laissez-faire by 1914?

2. Why was there a growth in democracy in Britain between 1860 and 1918?

3. How big an impact did the Labour Movement have on British politics and society by 1924?

4. To what extent did opportunities for women improve between 1900 and 1979?

5. "The social reforms of the Labour government of 1945–1951 were successful in establishing a welfare state." Do you agree?

### Section (b): The Growth of Nationalism

6. **Either**

   Compare the influence of nationalism, economic factors and political leadership in the achievement of German unification.

   **or**

   Do you agree that Cavour's role in the unification of Italy has been exaggerated?

7. **Either**

   How successfully did German foreign policy between 1871 and 1914 promote German interests?

   **or**

   How far do you accept the view that Italian foreign policy between 1870 and 1914 was dominated by the need to satisfy national pride?

8. **Either**

   "The economic depression of 1929–1932 was the turning point in Nazi fortunes." How well does this explain Hitler's achievement of power in 1933?

   **or**

   To what extent was Mussolini's rise to power made easy by Italy's economic and political difficulties?

9. **Either**

   How popular with the German people were Hitler's domestic policies between 1933 and 1939?

   **or**

   How far do you agree that Mussolini's domestic achievements between 1922 and 1939 were very limited?

## Section (c): The Large Scale State

### Answer on the USA OR Russia OR China

*The USA*

**10.** To what extent did ethnic minority groups suffer from racial discrimination in the USA during the 1920s?

**11.** How far were the economic problems faced by the USA in the 1930s due to the laissez-faire economic policies of Republican administrations during the 1920s?

**12.** "The work of the federal government, in promoting economic recovery through the New Deal, has been greatly exaggerated." How far do you accept this view?

**13.** "An inevitable response to white racism." Discuss this view of the emergence of black radical movements in the 1960s.

**OR**

*Russia*

**14.** Was the Tsarist state as strong as it appeared before 1905?

**15.** How effectively did Stolypin maintain the authority of the Tsarist state in the years after 1905?

**16.** To what extent did the First World War cause the downfall of the Tsarist state?

**17.** Why were the Bolsheviks successful in establishing their authority over Russia between 1917 and 1921?

**OR**

*China*

**18.** Why did the power of the imperial government collapse so quickly in 1911?

**19.** Why did the government of Jiang Jieshi (Chiang Kai-shek) fail to maintain its authority over China?

**20.** How far did the "Great Proletarian Cultural Revolution" weaken central authority in China?

**21.** "Superpower or Third World Country." Which, in your opinion, is the more accurate description of China in the 1970s and 1980s?

[*END OF QUESTION PAPER*]

SCOTTISH CERTIFICATE OF EDUCATION 1999

THURSDAY, 13 MAY
1.30 PM – 3.30 PM

# HISTORY
## HIGHER GRADE
Paper II
Sources

| *Option* | | *Special Topic* |
|---|---|---|
| **A Medieval History** | 1 | Norman Conquest and Expansion 1050–1153 |
| | 2 | The Crusades 1096–1204 |
| | 3 | Trade and Towns |
| **B Early Modern History** | 4 | Scotland 1689–1715 |
| | 5 | The Atlantic Slave Trade |
| | 6 | The American Revolution |
| | 7 | The Enlightenment in Scotland |
| **C Later Modern History** | 8 | Patterns of Migration: Scotland 1830s–1930s |
| | 9 | The Third French Republic 1871–1914 |
| | 10 | African Societies and European Imperialism 1880–1914 |
| | 11 | Appeasement and the Road to War, to 1939 |
| | 12 | The Origins and Development of the Cold War 1945–1985 |
| | 13 | Ireland 1900–1985: a Divided Identity |

## SPECIAL TOPIC 1: NORMAN CONQUEST AND EXPANSION 1050–1153

**Study the sources below and then answer the questions in the accompanying question paper.**

**Source A:** from *The Deeds of William, Duke of the Normans and King of the English,* written *c.*1071 by William of Poitiers.

On their return [from Brittany] Duke William kept his favoured guest [Harold] with him a little longer before letting him go, laden with gifts which were worthy both of him [Edward] by whose command he had come and him [William] whose honour he had come to increase. In addition, his nephew, one of the two hostages, was released for his sake to return with him. Therefore we address these words to you, Harold. How, after these things, do you dare to rob William of his inheritance and wage war upon him whom by sacred oath you have recognised as of your race, and to whom you have committed yourself by hand and mouth?

**Source B:** from the Song of the Battle of Hastings, probably written before 1070.

The French, skilled in warfare, pretended to flee as if defeated. The English peasantry rejoiced and believed they had won; they pursued in the rear with naked swords. But those who feigned flight turned on the pursuers . . . The flight which had first been a ruse became enforced by the English attack. The Normans fled; their shields covered their backs!

When the duke saw his people retreat vanquished, he rushed to confront the rout. Raging, he himself bared his head of the helmet. To the Normans he showed a furious countenance—to the French he spoke words of entreaty. Their faces grew red with shame. They wheeled, turned to face the enemy. The duke, as leader, was the first to strike; after him the rest laid on. Coming to their senses, they regained strength by scorning fear.

**Source C:** from the *Ecclesiastical History* of Orderic Vitalis, written between *c.*1114 and 1141.

After the king's return from Normandy, 1068, he was at great pains to appease everyone . . . Every city and district which he had visited in person or occupied with his garrison obeyed his will. But in the marches of his kingdom, to the west and north, the inhabitants were still barbarous, and had only obeyed the English king in the time of King Edward and his predecessors, when it suited their ends. Exeter was the first town to fight for liberty, but fell vanquished before the valiant forces that fiercely assaulted it . . .

The king commanded the leading citizens to swear fealty to him. But they sent back the following message, "We will neither swear fealty nor admit him within our walls; but we will pay tribute to him according to ancient custom". The king in his turn replied as follows, "It is not my custom to have subjects on such terms". Thereupon he marched on them in force, and for the first time called out Englishmen in his army.

Finally the citizens were compelled by the unremitting attacks of the enemy to take wiser counsel and humbly plead for pardon. The flower of their youth, the older men and the clergy bearing their sacred books and treasures went out to their king. As they humbly threw themselves on his mercy that just prince graciously granted them pardon and forgave their guilt, deliberately overlooking the fact that they had wantonly resisted him, and had insulted and ill-treated certain knights sent by him from Normandy, who had been driven by storm into their harbour . . . The king refrained from seizing their goods and posted a strong and trustworthy guard at the gates, so that the rank and file of the army could not suddenly break in and loot the city.

**Source D:** from B. Golding, *Conquest and Colonisation* (1994).

By 1070 William must have realised that his policy of creating a genuine Anglo-Norman state was unrealisable, and from now on change would be by imposition not agreement. It is only at this point, according to Orderic, that wholesale reallocation of honours took place, with the consequence of further unrest. The risings of 1070 and 1071 were the result of resented confiscations of land.

**Source E:** Map of castles built by William the Conqueror.

**Source F:** from F.M. Stenton, *Anglo-Saxon England* (1971).

But in spite of these and many other points of continuity, the fact remains that sooner or later every aspect of English life was changed by the Norman Conquest . . . To the ordinary Englishman who had lived from the accession of King Edward to the death of King William, the Conquest must have seemed an unqualified disaster. It is probable that, as a class, the peasants had suffered less than those above them. Many individuals must have lost life or livelihood at the hands of Norman raiders, and many estates had been harshly exploited in the interests of Norman lords anxious for ready money. But the structure of rural society was not seriously affected by the Norman settlement. To the thegnly class the Conquest brought not only the material consequences of an unsuccessful war, but also loss of privilege and social consideration. The thegn of 1066 who made his peace with the Conqueror lived thenceforward in a strange and unfriendly environment.

**Source G:** from D. Walker, *The Normans in Britain* (1995).

For Scotland, the concept of colonisation must be changed; what has served elsewhere in Britain will not stand. Geoffrey Barrow is fully committed to the view that there was a large-scale process of colonisation. An Anglo-Norman aristocracy was introduced into and endowed in Scotland, and Le Patourel's "aristocratic colonisation" can be identified. At a lower level of society there was substantial Flemish and English settlement and the planting of alien communities to exploit the country's natural resources is plain to see. But we shall find no conquest and no exploitation for the benefit of a foreign homeland.

*[END OF SOURCES FOR SPECIAL TOPIC 1]*

## SPECIAL TOPIC 2: THE CRUSADES 1096–1204

**Study the sources below and then answer the questions in the accompanying question paper.**

**Source A:** from Ibn al Athir, *The Sum of World History*, written in the early thirteenth century.

In 1186 Raymond of Tripoli began a correspondence with Saladin, established a cordial relationship with him and turned to him for help in achieving his ambition to rule the Franks. Saladin and the Moslems were pleased and Saladin promised to help him and to give him every possible assistance in his plans. He guaranteed to make him king of all the Franks. He freed some of the count's knights whom he held prisoner, which made the best possible impression on Raymond, who openly displayed his obedience to Saladin. A certain number of Franks followed his example, which led to discord and disunity, and was one of the chief reasons why their towns were reconquered and Jerusalem fell to the Moslems.

**Source B:** Philip's departure from Acre, according to the *Chronicle* of Rigord, a French monk, written between 1180 and 1196.

What provisions were found [at Acre] the Christians divided among themselves, giving a greater share to the many and a lesser to the few. But the kings had all the captives for their part and divided them equally. The king of France however handed over his half to the duke of Burgundy, together with much gold and silver and an infinite quantity of provisions. To the same duke he also entrusted his armies. For he was then sick of a very grievous illness, and besides this looked upon the king of England with much suspicion because the latter king was sending envoys to Saladin and giving and receiving gifts.

**Source C:** Description of a Moslem raid on the kingdom of Jerusalem in 1182, from *A History of Deeds Beyond the Sea* by William, archbishop of Tyre, who died in 1183.

[The Christian army was paralysed in 1182] through hatred of the count of Jaffa [Guy of Lusignan] to whom, two days before, the king of Jerusalem [Baldwin] had entrusted the welfare of the kingdom. For [the barons] took it ill that at so critical and dangerous a time matters of the highest importance had been placed in the hands of an obscure man, wholly incapable and indiscreet. As a result they disgracefully allowed the enemy to remain for eight successive days encamped in the vicinity of our army hardly more than [one kilometre] away—a thing which, it is said, had never happened before in the kingdom. During this time the Turks ravaged the entire region without fear of punishment.

**Source D:** from J. Riley-Smith, *The Crusades, a Short History* (1990).

Richard was not nearly as successful in local politics as he was on the battlefield. His support of Guy of Lusignan, to whom he was prepared to surrender his conquests, was frustrated by Conrad of Montferrat, the French crusaders and the local barons, who had never really accepted the compromise of 28 July 1191.

Richard came to realise that Guy's political situation was hopeless and *c.* 13 April he summoned a council of his army and accepted the advice that Conrad should be king.

**Source E:** from J. Riley-Smith, *The Crusades, a Short History* (1990).

Within a fortnight, Conrad was dead, struck down in Tyre by Assassins. It was never known who had employed them, but the seizure of Richard as he returned from the crusade by Leopold of Austria, who had taken part in the siege of Acre, and his imprisonment by the emperor Henry VI demonstrates that they, who were both Conrad's cousins, believed that he had been responsible. At any rate Isabella was now married, with Richard's consent if not on his initiative, to the crusader Count Henry of Champagne, who ruled the kingdom until his death in 1197.

**Source F:** the assassination of Conrad, from T. Jones and A. Ereira, *Crusades* (1996).

The most obvious beneficiary [of the murder] was Henry of Champagne and he turned up at Tyre as soon as he heard of the assassination—to be acclaimed immediately by the populace as their new lord and the man who should marry the newly widowed (and pregnant) Isabella. He was young, popular and the nephew of both Richard and Philip. He and Isabella were married within forty-eight hours of the murder. Richard approved. But although Henry ruled as a king, he was never crowned. No-one knows why.

The chroniclers do not devote many lines to merchants and seamen; they are impressed by knightly valour and religious fervour, not account books and sordid squabbles over money. But it is clear that the other main beneficiaries of Conrad's death were the Pisans. Richard and Henry now confirmed them in privileges which gave them control over the whole of the economically important section of Acre. This was still not enough for them and the following year a Pisan plot was discovered in which Tyre would be seized by force and Guy of Lusignan brought back from Cyprus to rule it. Henry banned all Pisans from his kingdom.

**Source G:** Richard's attack on Jaffa in 1192, from *The Itinerary of Richard I,* written in the early thirteenth century.

The word was forthwith given, the galleys were pushed to land. The king dashed forward into the waves with his thighs unprotected by armour, and up to his middle in water . . . The Turks stood to defend the shore, which was covered with their numerous troops. The king, with a crossbow which he held in his hand, drove them back right and left. His companions pressed upon the recoiling enemy, whose courage quailed when they saw it was the king . . . The king brandished his fierce sword, which allowed them no time to resist, but they yielded before his fiery blows, and were driven in confusion with blood and havoc by the king's men until the shore was entirely cleared of them . . . The brave king had no sooner entered the town, than he caused his banners to be hoisted on high, that they might be seen by the Christians in the tower, who taking courage at the sight rushed forth in arms from the tower to meet the king, and at the report thereof, the Turks were thrown into confusion. The king, meanwhile, with brandished sword still pursued and slaughtered the enemy, who were thus enclosed between the two bodies of the Christians, and filled the streets with their slain.

**Source H:** from R.H.C. Davis, *A History of Medieval Europe* (1970).

The whole conduct of the Third Crusade had belied the intentions of idealists such as Urban II or St. Bernard. They had promised the crusaders a plenary indulgence for their sins, because they had regarded a Crusade as a religious exercise or pilgrimage in arms. They had thought that those who took the Cross would, like those who took the cowl, renounce their worldly jealousies and former enmities for the sake of Christ. In fact they had merely transferred them from Europe to Palestine, and had defiled the Holy Land with their wickedness. Younger sons who had no land in Europe would make a career out of crusading, and would, if they were lucky, end up with a lordship or principality. Italian cities which lent their fleets, did so in return for concessions which would assist their trade. Crusading, far from being a religious exercise, had become an enterprising way of making one's fortune.

[*END OF SOURCES FOR SPECIAL TOPIC 2*]

## SPECIAL TOPIC 3: TRADE AND TOWNS

**Study the sources below and then answer the questions in the accompanying question paper.**

**Source A:** A.A.M. Duncan, *Scotland, the Making of the Kingdom* (1975).

Why towns at all? . . . The markets at Kelso and Brechin villages were examples of rural markets which probably existed widely but without the recognition and organisation achieved by these two exceptions. The market monopolies of burghs arose from a wish to end the rivalry from such landward exchanges.

The restrictions imposed by the state and by the dominant landowning group upon rural society, on succession to land among the landowners, on personal freedom (to move, to own and to contract) among the peasantry, were essentially contrary to the aims of men seeking to profit by trafficking. They must be free of restrictions on their means of livelihood, must be outside the feudal order of landward areas, and must develop their own rules of personal status, ownership, succession and trafficking. For these reasons, men took to the collective security of towns and developed a way of life sometimes viewed with suspicion by some feudatories.

**Source B:** from H.L. MacQueen and W.L. Windram, "Law Courts in the Burghs", in M. Lynch, M. Spearman and G. Stell (eds.), *The Scottish Medieval Town* (1988).

It is common to present this law of the burghs as distinct from the law of the realm and to state that the difference arose because burgesses as traders needed to escape from the "feudal" restrictions on landownership and freedom of movement in order to carry on their trading activities properly. Such a presentation is derived from an outmoded approach to medieval burghs which emphasised the development of urban liberties and privileges as a result of a struggle to escape from the power of magnates in the countryside. But this cannot be convincingly applied to Scotland, where military feudalism and burghs arrived together and spread together under the patronage and encouragement of successive kings from the twelfth century on. Indeed, far from engaging in a struggle with the burgesses, magnates of the twelfth and thirteenth centuries seem to have been eager to establish their own burghs at places such as Kirkintilloch, Prestwick and Dunbar.

**Source C:** from the records of the burgh council of Edinburgh, 10 November 1492.

It is ordered that no craftsman or indweller in the town should have the freedom of the town by practising their craft unless they are free burgesses or unless they are stall holders for the year who pay their dues to the clerk. This statute is to be extended to apply to all manner of unfree folk, traders, brewsters, baxters, regraters of fish, butter, cheese, eggs, wild fowl and other things.

**Source D:** from the records of the burgh court of Peebles, 21 January 1459.

The bailies, William of Peebles and Tom Dixon with the dozen and with the eldest of the town met in John Small's house to consider certain matters concerning the town and Holy Kirk.

Sir John Helston for the High Kirk claimed 4s annual rent from the east side of the land of Matthew Hutteris. Sir Adam Foster for the Cross Kirk claimed that the 4s annual rent belonged to the Cross Kirk. This, he said, had been decided previously by the eldest and best along with the chosen dozen.

Sir John denied this and said the matter had never gone to assize nor inquest nor had men sworn to it. The bailies and the good men then asked the parties to leave. The dozen and the eldest of the town decided that the 4s worth of annual rent should go to the Cross Kirk as it was decided previously. Sir John was ordered to cease because the High Kirk had no right to the annual rent according to the document and knowledge of the eldest of the good town.

**Source E:** from W.C. Dickinson, G. Donaldson and I.A. Milne, *A Source Book of Scottish History*, vol. 2 (1958).

Already the freemen in the burghs were distinguished as being either merchants (buyers and sellers) or craftsmen (makers). In the fifteenth and sixteenth centuries the merchants—possibly because they were the wealthier class, possibly because their trading activities brought greater benefit to the burghs and the realm, possibly because the organisation of trade and the organisation of the burgh were so closely interrelated—gradually acquired . . . complete control of burghal government . . . In 1504 all officers and magistrates were to be chosen from those using merchandise—ie merchants. By successive acts offices and power were gradually concentrated in the hands of the merchants and, where the act of 1469 became operative, power was further concentrated in the hands of a small group of merchants who elected their own members to office year by year. Such a monopoly of power soon led to corruption.

**Source F:** from J. Gilbert, "Selkirk in the Fourteenth and Fifteenth Centuries", in J. Gilbert (ed.), *The Flowers of the Forest* (1985).

Firstly, suppose that David II's charter were applied [in Selkirk]. One has to assume that any farmer or royal huntsman going to Selkirk market had to sell his hides to a merchant and that the cordiner or souter, tanner or leather worker had to buy those hides from the merchants. This applied not only to hides but to all merchandise. In a town of 500 this is clearly unworkable.

The act of 1469 entitling the crafts to elect one person to help elect the burgh officials is supposed to have led to the crafts getting the burghs to grant them incorporations sealed with the burgh court seal of cause . . . The reason, perhaps, why the crafts did not rush to get their incorporations in Selkirk after 1469 was presumably because they did not need to do so. They must already have had sufficient say in running the town and electing officials. The merchants may not have dominated the town, and may not even have had a guild . . . It would seem reasonable to assume that craftsmen were allowed to buy and sell without going through a merchant, and that there was no distinction between merchants and craftsmen since many individuals were, in fact, both.

**Source G:** from an act of Parliament in 1427.

The laws made in preceding parliaments about deacons of craftsmen in the burghs have led to the harm and common loss of the whole realm. The king, therefore, has . . . annulled these laws and forbids such deacons to be elected. He also orders those craft deacons already elected not to exercise their office and not to make their accustomed meetings which are presumed to savour of conspiracies.

[*END OF SOURCES FOR SPECIAL TOPIC 3*]

## SPECIAL TOPIC 4: SCOTLAND 1689–1715

**Study the sources below and then answer the questions in the accompanying question paper.**

**Source A:** from William Seton of Pitmedden, *A Speech in Parliament on the first article of the Treaty of Union* (1706).

The people and government of Scotland must be richer or poorer, as they have plenty or scarcity of money, the common measure of trade . . .

This nation is behind all other nations of Europe for many years, with respect to the effects of an extended trade.

This nation, being poor and without force to protect its commerce, cannot reap great advantages by it, till it partake of the trade and protection of some powerful neighbour nation, that can communicate both of these . . .

My Lord, I'm sorry that in place of things we amuse ourselves with words; for my part I comprehend no durable Union betwixt Scotland and England, but that expressed in this Article, that is to say, one people, one civil government and one interest.

'Tis true, the words Federal Union are become very fashionable, and may be handsomely fitted to delude unthinking people. But if any member of this House will give himself the trouble to examine what conditions or Articles are understood by these words, and reduce them to any kind of federal compacts, whereby distinct nations have been united, I'll presume to say, these will be found impracticable, or of very little use to us.

**Source B:** from Daniel Defoe, *The History of the Union between England and Scotland* (1709).

The former notion of a federal union had upon all occasions been found impracticable. It would entirely have left both nations exposed to the possibility of relapsing into a divided condition. It could not be expected that England, whose considerations for uniting were peace, strength and shutting a back door of continual war and confusion from the north, should communicate trade, freedom of customs in all her ports and plantations, with import and export of manufactures, and leave the main things yet precarious and uncertain.

**Source C:** a resolution put forward in the Scottish Parliament by the duke of Hamilton, 17 July 1705.

That this Parliament will not proceed to the nomination of a successor till we have had a previous Treaty with England in relation to our commerce and other concerns with that nation. And further, it is resolved, that this Parliament will proceed to make such limitations and conditions of government . . . as may secure the liberty, religion and independence of this kingdom before they proceed to the said nomination.

**Source D:** from K.M. Brown, *Kingdom or Province? Scotland and the Regal Union* (1992).

The treaty bargained Scottish political independence for economic dependence . . . The enlarged English parliament would contain forty-five members of parliament from Scotland (a 12:1 ratio) and sixteen representative peers. This low representation flattered the nation's economic strength (38:1) at a time when wealth was equated with political power, but grossly under-represented the population ratio (5:1) between the two kingdoms. However, fifteen of the twenty-five articles were concerned with economic issues. The Scots were assured of free trade with England and her colonies, fulfilling the ambitions of those who believed an expanded market was the only route to prosperity . . . To compensate for the existing English national debt, concessions were made to the Scots over the implementation of the salt and malt taxes, they were made to pay a lower rate on the land tax, and were to be exempted from other taxes, like that on stamped paper and windows. The equivalent, a sum almost £398,000 sterling, would be provided to pay off the debts of the crown in Scotland, chiefly to office holders, and to compensate investors in the Company of Scotland. A second, arising, equivalent would be made available as a start-up for Scottish industry.

**Source E:** from Christopher Whatley, *Bought and Sold for English Gold?* (1994).

The significance of the Squadrone Volante requires to be emphasised . . . There were, roughly speaking, three party groupings in the pre-1707 Parliament. Just the largest, the Court Party, included the officers of state and other London-appointees and acted and governed on behalf of the monarch. The opposition comprised the Country Party and the smaller Cavalier Party, whose members were effectively Jacobites, who wanted to restore the Stuart line. A "New Party", which became known as the Squadrone Volante, an off-shoot of the Country Party, was formed in 1704, led by the marquess of Tweeddale. Although anxious to promote an image of political reasonableness and concern for Scotland's future, this was misleading. The support of the two dozen or so members of the Squadrone Volante was vital to the Court. They held the balance, and without their votes, as has long been recognised, the union could not have succeeded. Their support for the incorporating union represented a major shift of position.

**Source F:** map showing addresses against the union, from P. McNeill and H. MacQueen (eds.), *An Atlas of Scottish History* (1996).

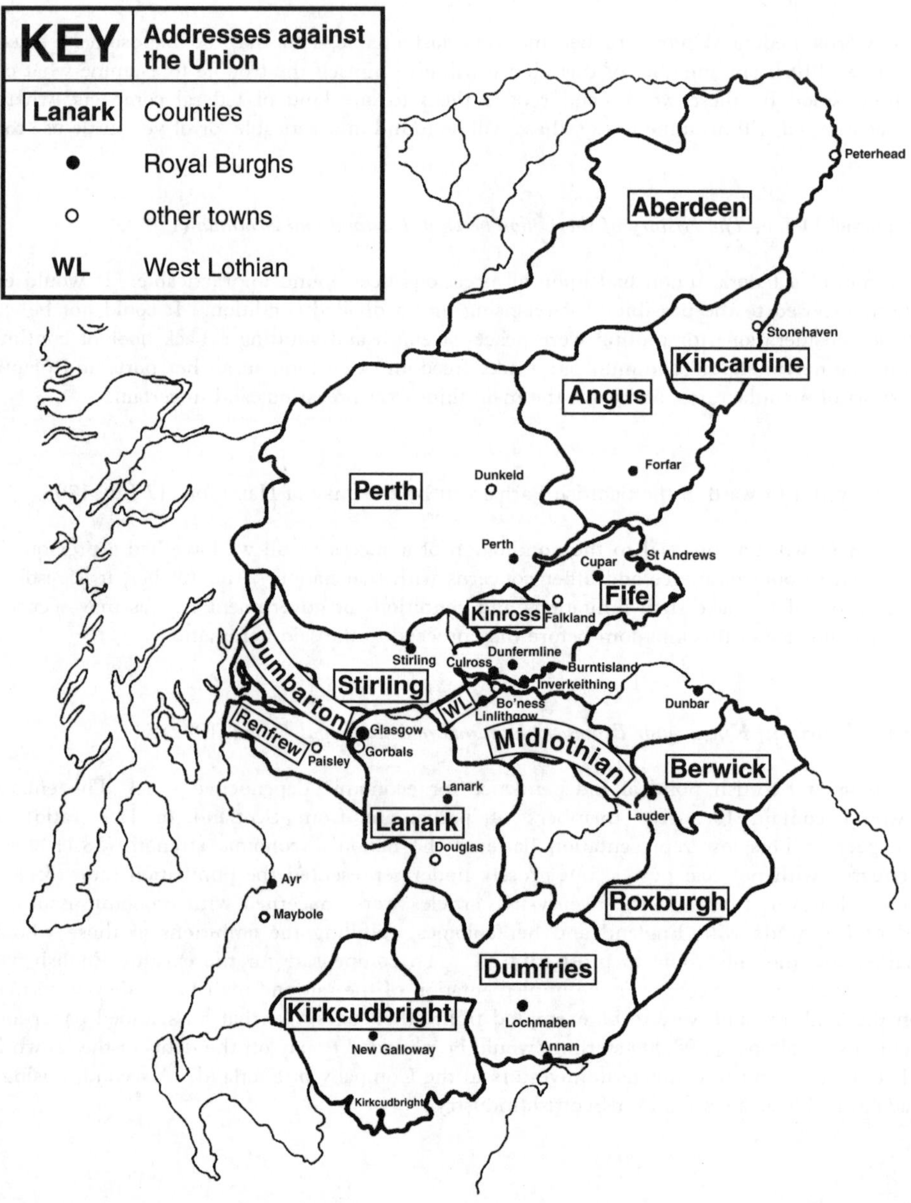

**Source G:** from R.A. Houston and I.D. Whyte, *Scottish Society 1500–1800* (1989).

In a letter to Robert Harley dated 24 October 1706, Daniel Defoe referred to troubles within the Scots parliament and to street protests. A few days later a mob attending Hamilton on a visit to the duke of Atholl set to Patrick Johnston's door. His wife called out of the window for the city guard but a bystander who tried to summon them "found the officers very indifferent in the matter, whether as to the cause or through fear of the rabble". The mob withdrew when the guard eventually arrived but "they fled not far, but shouting and throwing stones and sticks at the soldiers". In the evening of that day, the riot flared up again and Defoe "saw a terrible multitude come up the High Street with a drum at the head of them, shouting and swearing and crying out all Scotland would stand together, no Union, no Union, English dogs and the like". The city's ports were shut but crowds continued to throng the city.

**Source H:** from I. Donnachie and G. Hewitt (eds.), *A Companion to Scottish History from the Reformation to the Present* (1989)

OGILVIE, James, first earl of Seafield (1644–1730).

Originally a Jacobite at the start of William III's reign, he was soon won over by the Crown and remained a loyal servant until the Treaty of Union. As Secretary of State he performed sterling service at the height of the crisis involving the Company of Scotland and again in the reign of Queen Anne during the events leading towards the Union. As Chancellor in 1702–1704 and 1705–1707 he played a major part in furthering the interest of the Queen and her ministers. The ultimate outcome owed a great deal to his efforts and he was suitably rewarded by a grateful English government. Latterly, resentment at the abolition of the Privy Council, annoyance at the decision preventing the admission of Scots peers with English titles to the House of Lords and the introduction of the Malt Tax in Scotland made Seafield increasingly disaffected. Thus, in 1713, he took the lead in moving the bill for the repeal of the Treaty of Union. In 1715 he displayed a certain amount of sympathy for the Jacobites but astutely avoided any open commitment to the cause.

[*END OF SOURCES FOR SPECIAL TOPIC 4*]

## SPECIAL TOPIC 5: THE ATLANTIC SLAVE TRADE

**Study the sources below and then answer the questions in the accompanying question paper.**

**Source A:** from Olaudah Equiano, *Narrative of his life* (1792).

I was soon put down under the decks, and there I received such a smell in my nostrils as I had never experienced in my life. With the loathsomeness of the stench, and crying together, I became so sick and low that I was not able to eat, nor had I the least desire to taste anything. I now wished for the last friend, death, to relieve me; but soon, to my grief, two white men offered me eatables. On my refusing to eat, one of them held me fast by the hands and laid me across I think the windlass, and tied my feet, while the other flogged me severely. I had never experienced any thing of this kind before. Although not being used to the water, I naturally feared that element the first time I saw it, nevertheless could I have got over the nettings, I would have jumped over the side, but I could not. Besides, the crew used to watch us very closely who were not chained down to the decks, lest we should leap into the water. I have seen some of these poor African prisoners most severely cut for attempting to do so, and hourly whipped for not eating. This indeed was often the case with myself. In a little time after, amongst the poor chained men, I found some of my own nation. I inquired of these what was to be done with us; they gave me to understand we were to be carried to these white people's country to work for them.

**Source B:** a cartoon published in London in 1792.

*The ABOLITION of the SLAVE TRADE*

**Source C:** from J.R. Oldfield, *Popular Politics and British Anti-Slavery* (1995).

The American revolution gave slavery political meaning. But it also had a more far-reaching effect . . . One of the results of the loss of the American colonies was a move to tighten the reins of empire elsewhere, in Canada and Ireland. Another, however, was "a rise in enthusiasm for parliamentary reform . . . for religious liberalisation, for the reform of gaols and lunatic asylums; for virtually anything, in fact, that might prevent a similar national humiliation in the future". Here, in other words, was the catalyst that abolitionists had been looking for. The American war came to an end in 1783. Four years later Sharp and his friends organised the Society for the Abolition of the Slave Trade. Can this have been coincidence?

**Source D:** from the *Derby Mercury*, 16 February 1792.

It has been said that a *Petition from the Ladies* to Parliament, for an Abolition of the Slave Trade, would have a good effect. The idea is certainly a proper one—for as *Female Misery* is included in the wretched allotment of the Africans, an appeal in their behalf from the same sex must carry great weight behind it.

**Source E:** from J.R. Oldfield, *Popular Politics and British Anti-Slavery* (1995).

The publishing strategy of the London Committee . . . reveals how effectively business and marketing skills were transferred to reform. Early efforts were concentrated on producing cheap promotional literature that could be distributed in large quantities through the Committee's country agents. Thomas Clarkson's *Summary View of the Slave Trade* (1788) and the Dean of Middleham's *Letter to the Treasurer of the Society instituted for the Purpose of effecting the Abolition of the Slave Trade* (1788) both fell into this category. Over 15,000 copies of each of these titles were printed for the Committee in the fifteen months up to August 1788 alone, and the final figure, particularly in the case of the *Letter*, was probably closer to 20,000. Running to just sixteen pages and small enough to pass easily from hand to hand, these publications, really short pamphlets, were intended to introduce readers to the subject of the slave trade and arouse their sympathy and interest . . .

The Committee also expended a great deal of time and energy on its subscription lists. Between June 1787 and August 1788 no fewer than four different lists were distributed throughout the country agents, each one of them longer and more detailed than the last. These lists of financial supporters were important, not simply because of the sums of money involved, but because of the information they supplied about the subscribers, their status, place of residence and so on . . . Subscribing to any type of project, cultural or otherwise, was a form of self-advertisement; it was helpful, therefore, to be able to recognise names one knew and respected, especially in one's own region or locality.

**Source F:** from Seymour Drescher, *Capitalism and Antislavery* (1986).

The total number of petitions rose from 102 in 1788 to 519 in 1792, the largest number ever submitted to the House on a single subject or in a single session. Every English county was now represented, although the most massive support still seemed to come from the North. In 1788 petitions from north of the Tweed had represented only corporate Scotland: presbyteries, synods, universities and a chamber of commerce. In 1792 Scotland arrived in full force: municipalities, parishes, professions and trades.

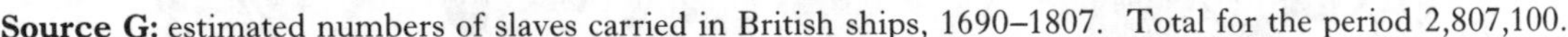

**Source G:** estimated numbers of slaves carried in British ships, 1690–1807. Total for the period 2,807,100.

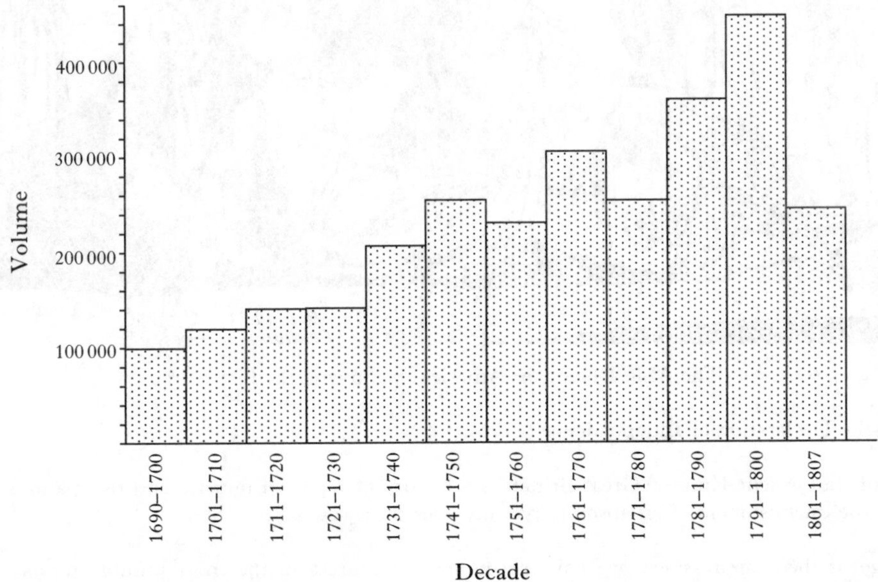


**Source H:** from a speech by Sir William Young in the House of Commons, 1806.

With the abolition of the Slave Trade, the value of West India property will be greatly diminished. I would put it to any gentleman in this House, that if he had laid out any large sum of money to the owners of any of the West India Plantations, he would immediately on the passing of this resolution, or any measure tending to the abolition of the African Slave Trade, demand his money back. He would think it insecure, if there were to be no more importation of slaves to cultivate those islands.

*[END OF SOURCES FOR SPECIAL TOPIC 5]*

## SPECIAL TOPIC 6: THE AMERICAN REVOLUTION

**Study the sources below and then answer the questions in the accompanying question paper.**

**Source A:** from S. Morison, H. Commager and W. Leuchtenberg, *A concise history of the American Republic* (1983).

The immense gains of the Seven Years War persuaded British statesmen that their bigger empire required more ships and soldiers. These would cost money; and unless the British taxpayer supplied it all, the colonies, which also benefitted, should contribute to the cost. Revenue could be extracted from the colonies only through a stronger central administration. As Governor Hutchinson of Massachusetts wrote, "There must be a limitation of so-called English Liberties in America". Furthermore, the Acts of Trade were strengthened to an extent that began to impose real hardships on important colonial interests.

**Source B:** an engraving from the *London Magazine*, 1774.

The Able Doctor, or America swallowing the bitter draught

**Source C:** from the Declaration of Independence (1776).

The history of the present King of Great Britain is a history of repeated injuries and usurpations, all having, in direct object, the establishment of an absolute tyranny over these states . . .

In every stage of these oppressions, we have petitioned for redress in the most humble terms. Our repeated petitions have been answered only by repeated injury. A Prince, whose character is thus marked by every act which may define a tyrant, is unfit to be the ruler of a free people.

**Source D:** a note from King George III to Lord North, 19 November 1774.

I return the private letters received from Lieut.-General Gage. His idea of suspending the Acts [the Intolerable Acts] appears to me the most absurd that can be suggested. The American people are ripe for mischief, yet he proposes that the mother country suspends the measures she has thought necessary. This must suggest to the colonies that we are afraid and this prompts them to their present violence. We must either master them or totally leave them to themselves and treat them as aliens. I do not by this mean to insinuate that I am for advising new measures, but I am for supporting those already undertaken.

**Source E:** from M.J. Heale, *The American Revolution* (1986).

When Tom Paine, an eloquent and insubordinate Englishman of modest birth, arrived in Philadelphia in 1774, he quickly became a spokesman for the radical intellectuals and artisans of that city. His celebrated book, *Common Sense,* published in January 1776, went well beyond the traditional Country complaints about a corrupt executive subverting the liberty of the people, and denounced the English constitution itself, with its basis in monarchical and aristocratic "tyranny". Paine agreed that Americans were threatened with slavery, but the problem was not so much corruption as the hereditary principle. It was not only George III himself who was at fault but all kings. Such notions could be turned against hierarchies of any kind, and there were mechanics and small farmers who concluded that their own liberty would be secured only in a truly egalitarian society. These men supported the removal of royal authority as the first step to this democratic end.

**Source F:** from the *Blackwell Encyclopaedia of the American Revolution* (1991).

Washington's main American army was not tested by its British counterpart in Boston—except in the bloody but inconclusive battle of Bunker Hill, which occurred before the Virginian's arrival in the Bay colony. Those months from July 1775 to March 1776 were crucial in two ways: one, Washington demonstrated that an American army need not be feared by its own citizens; and second, he had time to bring order and system to his command, as he watched the enemy from his well entrenched positions overlooking the city. Finally, William Howe, Gage's successor, sailed away on 17 March, preferring to regroup, await reinforcements and attack where the Americans seemed more vulnerable than in Massachusetts, the hotbed of American radicalism.

**Source G:** from J.R. Pole, *Foundations of American Independence* (1973).

If at that point the British had been capable of making anything resembling a correct military appraisal, and had sent an army of 200,000, as Gage had earlier demanded, instead of 20,000, and if they had shown any ability to muster the resources of the widely scattered but far-reaching support that existed in the American population, they might have won the war. But they now compounded their earlier mistakes. They had already underestimated the Americans, both in showing contempt for their courage and calibre and in failing to grasp the implications of a war against the people. Now they gave the American moderates no room to manoeuvre. The tougher the British line, the less chance the conservative leadership had to win an appeal for a reasonable reconciliation.

**Source H:** from the Constitution of the United States, 1787.

Article 1

Section 1 All legislative powers herein granted shall be vested in a Congress of the United States, which shall consist of a Senate and House of Representatives.

Section 2 The House of Representatives shall be composed of members chosen every second year by the people of the several states.

Article 10 The powers not delegated to the United States by the Constitution nor prohibited by it to the States, are reserved to the States respectively, or to the people.

[*END OF SOURCES FOR SPECIAL TOPIC 6*]

1999

## SPECIAL TOPIC 7: THE ENLIGHTENMENT IN SCOTLAND

**Study the sources below and then answer the questions in the accompanying question paper.**

**Source A:** from David Hume, *The History of Great Britain* (1761).

That security which the laws in Great Britain give to every man . . . was perfected by the revolution of 1688. In Great Britain industry is perfectly secure; and though it is far from being perfectly free, it is as free or freer than in any other part of Europe.

The revolution forms a new epoch in the constitution . . . And it may justly be affirmed, without any danger of exaggeration, that we, in this island, have ever since enjoyed, if not the best system of government, at least the most entire system of liberty that ever was known among mankind.

**Source B:** from Richard Teichgraber III, *Politics and Morals in the Scottish Enlightenment* (1978).

The most common mistake, especially outside Great Britain, is to regard Hume and Smith as two isolated geniuses and to consider them in the specialised context of philosophy and economics respectively. The first step towards a fuller understanding of the Scots is to realise that they were tied, by close personal contacts . . . to a larger group of men of letters with a common biographical pattern . . . They were almost all Lowland Scots: Hume and Kames came from Berwickshire, Smith was born at Kirkcaldy in Fife, Robertson at Dalkeith and Millar at Hamilton. The great majority of the Literati came from what we may call the middle classes: the small gentry (Hume, Monboddo, Kames), the urban bureaucracy (Smith), and the learned professions especially the clergy (Hutcheson, Ferguson, Robertson, Millar). They were educated at similar parish or burgh schools and went to the same universities, especially Edinburgh and Glasgow. As tutors to the sons of the aristocracy, most of them had travelled the Continent extensively. Eventually, they all settled, as professors (Hutcheson, Smith, Ferguson, Millar), lawyers (Kames, Monboddo) or clergymen (Robertson, Blair, A. Carlyle) at Glasgow or Edinburgh.

**Source C:** from Richard B. Sher, *Church and University in the Scottish Enlightenment* (1985).

In addition to appearing more impartial in regard to Mary, Queen of Scots, Robertson was widely believed to be a better writer and more thorough researcher than his rival. The *History of Scotland*, in short, was thought to come closer than Hume's work to the contemporary ideal of polite history, and its author was transformed almost overnight from a little-known provincial pastor into an international literary celebrity.

It would be difficult to exaggerate the importance of Robertson's book for advancing the cause of Moderatism and the Enlightenment in Scotland. Here was proof that a Scottish clergyman could make a name for himself in the republic of letters without compromising his church or his calling.

Robertson's stature after the *History of Scotland* is clear from the fact that his second historical work, the *History of Charles V*, earned him the staggering sum of £4000, by far "the greatest price that was ever known to be given for any book" (David Hume).

**Source D:** from Adam Smith, *The Wealth of Nations* (1776).

Man has almost constant occasion for the help of his brothers and it is vain for him to expect it from their benevolence only. He will be more likely to prevail if he can interest their self-love in his favour, and show them that it is for their own advantage to do for him what he requires of them . . . It is not from the benevolence of the butcher, the brewer or the baker, that we expect our dinner, but from their regard to their own interest. We address ourselves, not to their humanity but to their self-love, and never talk to them of our necessities, but of their advantage.

**Source E:** from David Hume, *Enquiry concerning the principle of morals* (1751).

It appears, that, in our general appreciation of characters and manners, the useful tendency of the social virtues moves us not by any regards to self interest, but has an influence much more universal and extensive. It appears that a tendency to public good, and to the promoting of peace, harmony and order in society does always, by affecting the benevolent principles of our frame, engage us on the side of the social virtues.

**Source F:** from Bruce Lenman, *Integration, Industrialisation and Enlightenment* (1992).

Robert Adam went on the Grand Tour as the companion of the Honourable Charles Hope, the younger brother of the Earl of Hopetoun. By this time it was very normal for Scottish aristocrats to participate in the extraordinary and expensive finishing school of the Grand Tour of Europe, devised originally for the sons of the English aristocracy. Variety was characteristic of the exercise but the itinerary of Robert Adam and Charles Hope gives a good idea of the elements which went into the Tour. From London they crossed the Channel to Calais, and after an excursion into the southern Netherlands they worked their way down from Paris to Marseilles and Nice whence they took ship for Genoa. Rome was the supreme treasure house of the artistic masterpieces on which the noble tourist was expected to form his taste, though there were usually plenty of Scots to be found enjoying the sights of the larger and livelier city of Naples further south.

**Source G:** from a translation of the Gaelic poem, *Song to the foxes* (for killing the sheep), written in the eighteenth century by Duncan ban Macintyre.

The villages and shielings
where warmth and cheer were found

have no houses save the ruins,
and no tillage in the fields.
Every practice that prevailed
in Gaeldom has been altered,

and become so unnatural in the places
that were hospitable.

**Source H:** from I. Donnachie and G. Hewitt (eds.), *A Companion to Scottish History from the Reformation to the Present* (1989).

GRANT, Sir Archibald of Monymusk (1696–1778).

Grant was the son of a distinguished Lord in Session, Lord Cullen, who was entrusted with his father's estate in Aberdeenshire about 1716 and soon became an energetic and persuasive advocate of agricultural improvement. Apart from duties as MP for Aberdeenshire, Grant devoted much of his time to the Monymusk estate, introducing enclosures, drainage, crop rotations, new grasses and root crops. At first many of his tenants resisted the changes. Some of the new fences and dykes on the estate were pulled down in night raids but Grant's apparently well-meaning paternalism prevailed—especially through the granting of long leases that gave the tenants an opportunity to benefit from the changes. Unlike many landowners he seems to have been motivated more by humanity than profit, to the extent that when John Wesley visited the district in 1761 he had nothing but praise for the social conditions of the people on Grant's estate.

[*END OF SOURCES FOR SPECIAL TOPIC 7*]

## SPECIAL TOPIC 8: PATTERNS OF MIGRATION: SCOTLAND 1830s–1930s

**Study the sources below and then answer the questions in the accompanying question paper.**

**Source A:** from "Inquiry into Vice and Destitution in Edinburgh", *Scotsman*, February 1850.

One cause of the difficulties which Protestant missionaries must feel in becoming acquainted with the wretched and the criminal population is the migratory habits of the people. This is one of the greatest obstacles in the way of bringing the power of the gospel and the good advice to bear on these unhappy creatures. But as these migrations are not to great distances, this will not account for their ignorance of the very names of missionaries and ministers. The Roman Catholics in the low localities are twice as well attended by their priests as the similar Protestants are. I found that absence from church was generally followed by a visit from the priest, and that the sick beds of his flock were not unattended. The priests of Rome everywhere do their duty to their church.

**Source B:** from S.G. Checkland, *The Upas Tree* (1976).

The Church of Scotland and the United Presbyterian Church could be regarded as to some extent unifying forces within Glasgow society, with all or most of their members aware of the dignity and sometimes formidableness of the minister as he bore witness to the duties of men and women to one another and to God. The ministers of both churches would instil the virtues of self help, work and thrift, and would thus sponsor families in improving their condition. The Roman Catholic Church could perform less of this unifying function, for it had little coverage in the upper end of society. But in a sense it was in the more powerful position, for its members certainly went to church, and accepted a strong obedience.

**Source C:** photograph of the Saltmarket, Glasgow, in the 1860s.

**Source D:** from the *Ayr Advertiser*, quoted in the *Glasgow Herald*, 1849.

In visiting any of the minor towns or villages in the county of Ayr, the fact that the Irish have caused general deterioration is powerfully brought home to the visitors by the wretched appearances of once comfortable localities, where nothing but Irish squalor and wretchedness is now to be seen; by the appearance of a large bulk of the population; by the immense increase in the number of spirit dealers; in short by the entire departure of many of the most prominent of the pleasing characteristics of the old Scottish village.

**Source E:** from T.M. Devine, *Exploring the Scottish Past* (1995).

By the 1830s and 1840s some of the large towns in Scotland were approaching a social crisis of unprecedented proportions. Meaningful efforts at reform were not even contemplated until the 1840s. Not before the second half of the nineteenth century were some of the worst aspects of the urban problem effectively tackled. Much of Glasgow's notoriety as the unhealthiest city in Britain at this time stemmed from the simple fact that it was growing more swiftly than any other British city of its size. It must also be remembered that the larger Scottish towns, especially those in the western Lowlands and Dundee, played host to migrants from Ireland and parts of the Highlands, two of the poorest societies in the British Isles. The Irish, in particular, often arrived in a semi-destitute condition, concentrated in the poorest quarters of the towns, were more vulnerable to the diseases of the city and inevitably aggravated pressure on accommodation and amenity.

**Source F:** from J.B. Russell, *The Vital Statistics of Glasgow* (1886).

We began this survey of the districts of Glasgow with Blythswood, which was remarkable as having the lowest population of inmates per inhabited room, the largest proportion of large-sized houses, the lowest death rate, the lowest birth rate, the lowest mortality under five years, the lowest proportion of deaths under one year per 1,000 born, and the lowest proportion of Irish born. We end it with Bridgegate and Wynds, which has the largest proportion of inmates per inhabited room, the largest proportion, save one, of one-apartment houses, the highest death rate over all, the highest death rate under five years, the largest proportion of deaths under one year per 1,000 born, and the highest proportion of Irish born inhabitants.

**Source G:** from a letter signed "Hibernicus" to the *Dundee Advertiser*, reprinted in the *Glasgow Free Press*, 1 February 1862.

No sooner has the initiative of the reading rooms project been fairly taken than the Catholic clergymen, those from whom above all others we expected sympathy, launch forth the thunders of the pulpit against us. And why do they condemn our reading rooms? Simply because they are not under their immediate control, because the promoters did not ask their permission, because the books, newspapers etc. are not under their immediate censorship, and because they are of a secular and educational tendency. We hold secular education to be as necessary as secular labour and some of our time may be as usefully spent in secular reading as in the recital of prayers.

**Source H:** from T.M. Devine (ed.), *Irish Immigrants and Scottish Society in the Nineteenth and Twentieth Centuries* (1991).

The state refused to make any financial provision for any Catholic education or social services . . . Along with systematic discrimination and the defensiveness of their own community, educational backwardness may help to explain why Catholics had a poor position in the labour market. This made it difficult for members of the community to identify themselves as part of a wider Scottish community. The reluctance of the immigrants to sacrifice their sense of community by following the Scottish route of self improvement which education provided, did not endear them to Scots who had other reasons to feel that the Catholic Irish were unworthy of equal status. Their religion was viewed as subversive and hostility towards them was reflected in police behaviour and in the courts. This increased the defensiveness and isolation of the immigrants.

[*END OF SOURCES FOR SPECIAL TOPIC 8*]

## SPECIAL TOPIC 9: THE THIRD FRENCH REPUBLIC 1871–1914

**Study the sources below and then answer the questions in the accompanying question paper.**

**Source A:** illustration of the Pas de Calais miners' strike from *Le Petit Journal*, 1906.

**Source B:** from the General Programme of the Socialist Regional Congress of the Centre, 18–23 July 1880.

*Political Programme*

1. Abolition of all laws upon the press, meetings and associations.
2. Suppression of the religious budget and return to the nation of the properties belonging to the religious corporation.
3. General arming of the people.

*Economic Programme*

1. Cessation of labour for one day per week or legal prohibition for employers operating more than six days out of seven. Reduction of the working day to eight hours for adults. Prohibition of the working of children under 14 years in private factories and, from 14 to 18 years, reduction of the working day to six hours.
2. Legal minimum of wages.
3. Equality of wages for workers of the two sexes.
8. Suppression of the right enjoyed by employers to impose any penalty whatever upon their working men under the form of fines or deductions from their wages.
9. Revision of all contracts which have alienated public property (banks, railroads, mines etc.)

**Source C:** from B.H. Moss, *The Origins of the French Labour Movement 1830–1914* (1980).

French *syndicats* defended the immediate material interests of the trade in matters of wages, hours, apprenticeship and working conditions through the use of strikes and collective bargaining. Even offensive demands for higher wages, lower hours and the like were presented as measures of resistance in defence of the relative position of the trade in an expanding economy. But political repression and the constant influx of new workers prevented the formation of effective trade unions. Since they lacked power in the labour market, trade societies often appealed to the government to set hours and wages. The failure of effective trade unionism may have advanced the cause of socialism but it is probably equally true that the belief in socialism distracted workers from building more effective trade unions. Thus, socialism must be seen both as a consequence and a contributing cause of the failure of trade unionism.

**Source D:** from the Law of Separation of Church and State, 9 December 1905.

1. The Republic assures the liberty of conscience. It guarantees the free exercise of religions, subject only to the restrictions imposed in the interest of law and order.

2. The Republic neither recognises nor salaries nor subsidises any religion. In consequence, expenses relating to the exercise of religion shall be suppressed in the budgets of the state, departments and communes.

**Source E:** from the Papal Encyclical, 11 February 1906.

To the archbishops, bishops, clergy and people of France . . . Our soul is full of sorrow and our heart overflows with grief when our thoughts dwell upon you. How could it be otherwise, immediately after the publication of that Law which sunders violently the old ties that linked your nation with the Apostolic See?

You have seen the sanctity of Christian marriage outraged by legislative acts in formal contradiction with them and the schools and hospitals taken from church control. Clerics have been torn from their studies to be subjected to military service, the religious orders dispersed and their members for the most part reduced to the last stage of destitution. The Law hands over the administration and guardianship of religious worship not to the body divinely instituted by the Saviour, but to an association of lay persons. It must be apparent to you all, even at a first glance, that such regulations are offensive to the Church, and that they will infringe its rights and be at variance with its divine constitution.

Besides the injury which it inflicts on the interests of the Church, the new Law is destined to be most disastrous for your country. For undoubtedly it destroys union and accord.

**Source F:** from N. Ravitch, *The Catholic Church and the French Nation* (1990).

The separation of Church and State in 1905 was the work of anti-clericals who had long sought this objective. While it was debated in the spirit of taking revenge on a Church which had been continually associated with anti-republican movements, two important results of the Separation were as significant as they were perhaps unexpected. Firstly, the clerical issue was removed from the centre of French politics. Secondly, the Church became entirely dependent on its faithful laity for support, and it pursued a reconciliation with the conservative elites of France more resolutely than ever before. In a sense, then, the Separation furthered achievement of some of the objectives of the *Ralliement*. The Separation was the last act of an official, governmental anti-clericalism which sought the disciplining, not the ruination, of the Church. Except in the competition between lay education and that provided by the Church, the virulent issues between clericals and anti-clericals had been laid to rest.

**Source G:** from R.D. Anderson, *France 1870–1914: Politics and Society* (1977).

During the "belle époque", France was by contemporary European standards an open society with high social mobility, in which the barriers to talent were low. The ideals of Republicans and the educational system which they promoted were designed to encourage this openness, and surely deserve some of the credit for the brilliant achievements which are found in this period in so many fields.

[*END OF SOURCES FOR SPECIAL TOPIC 9*]

## SPECIAL TOPIC 10: AFRICAN SOCIETIES AND EUROPEAN IMPERIALISM 1880–1914

**Study the sources below and then answer the questions in the accompanying question paper.**

**Source A:** from J.M. Mackenzie, *The Partition of Africa* (1983).

The expansion of education in Europe led to a considerable increase in literacy, and this was exploited by colonial pressure groups but above all by the missions. The missions were very important in putting forward imperial ideas. Mission societies became convinced of their divine mission to convert the world, to save other people from what they saw to be "barbarism" and "savagery".

**Source B:** from a letter from the earl of Derby to W.A.G. Young, 26 December 1884.

The course of proceedings in Berlin has been very favourable, on the whole, to British interests on the west coast and Her Majesty's Government are well satisfied with the result. If Germany has gained something, Britain has gained much more, and Her Majesty's Government have no wish to dispute the German acquisitions, or the way in which they were obtained. In the interests of British traders, putting aside the question of international policy, it is best to treat the Germans in the most friendly way possible, and to drop all further controversy. I am happy to believe that, now that the first alarm is over, the most intelligent traders have made up their minds that they have nothing to fear from German rule, and that they only desire to see it become more and more of a reality.

These confidential instructions are not to be taken as implying that you are, in cases which may *hereafter* arise between your Government and the German representatives, to cease the assertion of British rights.

**Source C:** from J.D. Hargreaves, *Prelude to the Partition of West Africa* (1961).

The importance of the Berlin Conference has often been misrepresented and exaggerated. Diplomatically, though it seemed a significant novelty that France and Germany should jointly sponsor such a conference, their African interests proved to be widely divergent, and the idea of a Franco-German friendly understanding lapsed. Germany's belief that the continental powers had united in an anti-British league was a myth. Nor is it true that the Conference "partitioned Africa". Territorial questions were specifically excluded from the agenda and agreements were restricted to the coastal districts, virtually all of which were taken over by 1885. Such provisions of the Berlin Act, like its vague references to the abolition of slave dealing and to the welfare of the peoples of the Congo basin, had little practical effect on the coming partition of Africa.

**Source D:** cartoon by John Tenniel, *Punch*, 29 August 1885.

THE "IRREPRESSIBLE" TOURIST.
BISMARCK. "HA!—HA!—WHERE SHALL I GO NEXT?"

**Source E:** from P. Gifford and W. Rodger Louis (eds.), *Britain and Germany in Africa* (1967).

In 1885 the only serious African question facing the Foreign Secretary was Zanzibar. Salisbury's attitude toward this problem was shaped by his desire to align British policy with Germany's on European issues. Salisbury at first regarded Bismarck's colonial schemes as little more than a passing phase. He rightly believed Bismarck's true aim was financial profit for German businessmen, not colonial expansion by the German government. Salisbury doubted the economic value of east Africa; his views often differed from those of his permanent officials. As long as the Germans did not threaten British strategic interests, Salisbury was willing to buy German friendship by giving way on colonial questions. But Salisbury found Bismarck a difficult partner and his tolerant attitude to the Germans in east Africa did not produce all the results he hoped for.

**Source F:** from a speech by Lord Salisbury in Parliament, 14 February 1885.

It is our business in all these new countries to make smooth the paths for British commerce and British enterprise at a time when outlets for our commercial energies are being gradually closed. It is the first duty of the Government to spare no opportunity of opening fresh outlets for these energies, and I confess that not wholly, but in a great measure, this great undertaking of England with respect to Uganda has been taken . . . because it is a country of vast fertility. It is a matter of vital importance that British commerce should have free access to that country, free access to the whole of the upper valley of the Nile. There are four, if not five, Powers that are steadily advancing towards the upper waters of the Nile. There will be competition—I will use no stronger word—for the advantages which predominance in that region will confer.

See the splendid work Mr Rhodes has done in the southern end of Africa. He has obtained little from any British government, but he has laid the foundations of a splendid empire. Even the government of the Transvaal, hostile as it has been to us, is finding the presence of English activity all around them so strong that they are slowly giving way.

**Source G:** from a telegram sent by Governor Nathan of Kumasi, Gold Coast, to the Foreign Office, 1901.

Propose, after consultation with Resident in Kumasi, deportation of 17, and detention of 27, leaders of rising; and to issue proclamation of amnesty to cover all offenders, with exception of those persons in custody, which include murderers of Branscombe and others, and except a few tribal chiefs not yet arrested, who will be mentioned by name. Propose that tribute should be paid. All the chiefs here, including most in the country, have agreed to this. I do not propose additional tribute for last year's war, but the rebel tribes should be punished for this by not being allowed to carry guns, and by being forced to provide free labour for additional barracks and military posts, made necessary in their districts by their conduct. Propose to fill all vacant stools with men duly elected and recommended to me by Resident in Kumasi, as these essential for administration of country, and do not propose any alteration in ownership of lands. Most important points should be decided before departure of myself from Kumasi.

[*END OF SOURCES FOR SPECIAL TOPIC 10*]

## SPECIAL TOPIC 11: APPEASEMENT AND THE ROAD TO WAR, TO 1939

**Study the sources below and then answer the questions in the accompanying question paper.**

**Source A:** from an article in the *Daily Sketch*, 9 March 1936.

I should take Herr Hitler at his word . . . You cannot for ever keep German troops out of their own territory, and Herr Hitler has now done it without so much as a By-your-leave. It is a flagrant violation of the Treaty of Versailles, but that Treaty is already so tattered as to be unrecognisable. As it stands, it is impossible to enforce it without war, and, as no-one wants war, what happens to it is a question of good manners rather than of good politics . . . Unless the powers propose to turn the Germans out they might as well make a virtue of necessity, and regularise their action with as much good grace as they can command. There is talk of sanctions through the League of Nations, but sanctions are either a form of sulks, or else mean war.

Much the more important question is what Germany proposes to do now that she has got there. Herr Hitler . . . offers a twenty-five years Pact of Peace with France and Belgium, and swears by all his gods that he means it. I believe he does.

**Source B:** from Michael Bloch, *Ribbentrop* (1992).

The immediate reactions were all that Hitler could have desired. Both in England and France, the overwhelming public feeling was that Germany had done no more than 'march into her backyard', and that it would be criminal folly to oppose her by measures involving the slightest risk of war. At the same time, there was a serious split in the attitudes of the British and French Governments. The British wished above all to avoid trouble . . . The French, whose entire security was based on Versailles and Locarno, believed it was essential to put Hitler under some form of pressure to withdraw his forces; but they felt unable to act without the British.

**Source C:** from a report by the Chiefs of Staff, 1936.

We would at once emphasise that any question of war with Germany while we are heavily committed to the possibility of hostilities in the Mediterranean would be thoroughly dangerous . . .

We also draw attention to the fact that the provision of equipment for the defence of our coasts and ports at home has been placed in the lowest category of importance. At the moment, our coast defence artillery requires modernisation to a large extent, we have no anti-submarine defences for a number of our most important ports, and the number of our anti-aircraft guns and searchlights is quite inadequate to deal with the air threat from Germany.

**Source D:** from a report by Neville Chamberlain of discussions in the Foreign Policy Committee, 18 March 1938.

If Germany could obtain what she wanted by peaceful methods, there was no reason to suppose she would reject such a procedure in favour of one based on violence. It should be noted that throughout the Austrian adventure, Herr Hitler had studiously refrained from saying or doing anything to provoke us, and in small matters, such as the position of British subjects returning home from Austria, consideration had been shown. All this did not look as if Germany wished to antagonise us. On the contrary, it indicated a desire to keep on good terms with us.

**Source E:** from a speech by Sir Archibald Sinclair in the House of Commons, 14 March 1938.

During these recent crises in the affairs of the world, many of us have begged the Government to make a stand, and to stop the retreat of the Democracies against the advance of the Dictatorships, but Honourable Members have shouted "You want war. You must be careful". So . . . we see the Democracies still on the retreat before the Dictatorships. We see, through the hail of bombs . . . and the rumbling of tanks . . ., the tide of anarchy and confusion rising and engulfing civilisation.

**Source F:** cartoon by David Low, *Evening Standard*, September 1938.

*Chamberlain,* 'Mein Kampf'.

**Source G:** from the *Perthshire Advertiser*, 1 October 1938.

By his courage and his perseverance, Mr Neville Chamberlain stands out clear above all others as the man who saved the peace of the world. His return to London last evening from the fateful conference at Munich was in the nature of a triumph. The cheers of the large crowds which assembled to greet him were the vocal expression of the heartfelt relief of nearly all the people of Britain, ex-Servicemen who remember the last war, widows who lost their husbands, and whose sons are of military age.

What is most important is the fact that he has been successful in preserving the peace and preventing the slaughter of thousands, perhaps millions of people, none of whom desires war. Blessed be our Prime Minister, and blessed be the little country of Czechoslovakia which helped by its self-sacrifice to ensure that peace.

Mr Chamberlain has brought home with him a document signed by Herr Hitler and himself binding Germany and Great Britain to settle all problems by the method of consultation, and not by force. Surely we may rest our minds that the German Fuhrer will acknowledge a pact which will go far to ensure the future peace of Europe.

**Source H:** from C. J. Bartlett, *British Foreign Policy in the 20th Century* (1984).

Chamberlain approached the German question with strong convictions. Indeed, the very strength of his convictions was a weakness. Information was selected and interpreted to support his beliefs. Even if the Allied military position had been stronger, his overall aims would have been similar.

Above all, Chamberlain wanted a comprehensive settlement with Germany. He believed that perfect all-round justice was impossible in Central Europe and that the weaker peoples had to bow to the stronger. He also believed that the stronger had to demonstrate that their aims were limited, their methods in pursuit of revision reasonable and that their long term commitment to peace, arms limitation and international co-operation was genuine.

Unfortunately, it became all too easy for Chamberlain to make more and more concessions as he pursued the mirage of a satisfied Germany. Concessions, which seemed a small price to pay for peace, were in fact being made for worthless promises.

[*END OF SOURCES FOR SPECIAL TOPIC 11*]

1999

## SPECIAL TOPIC 12: THE ORIGINS AND DEVELOPMENT OF THE COLD WAR 1945–1985

**Study the sources below and then answer the questions in the accompanying question paper.**

**Source A:** from a radio broadcast by E. Gero (Hungarian Prime Minister), 23 October 1956.

Dear Comrades, Beloved Friends, Working People of Hungary!
The enemies of the people . . . are trying to loosen the ties between our party and the glorious Communist Party of the Soviet Union, the party of Lenin, the party of the 20th Congress. They slander the Soviet Union.

We are not nationalists. We are waging a constant fight against anti-Semitism and all other reactionary, anti-social and inhuman trends and views. Therefore, we condemn those who try to spread these poisons among our youth, and who use the democratic freedom which our state has assured the working people for nationalistic demonstrations.

The unity of the Party, working-class and working people, must be guarded as the apple of our eye. Let our Party organisations oppose with discipline and complete unity any attempt to create disorder and provocation.

**Source B:** from a broadcast by Imre Nagy (Hungarian Prime Minister), 30 October 1956.

The National Government, in full agreement with the Praesidium of the Hungarian Workers' Party [Communist Party], has decided to take a step vital for the future of the whole nation, and of which I want to inform the Hungarian working people. The cabinet abolishes the one-party system and places the country's Government on the basis of democratic co-operation between coalition parties as they existed in 1945 . . . Hungarian brothers, workers and peasants: Rally behind the Government in this fateful hour! Long live free, democratic and independent Hungary!

**Source C:** from G. Litvan (ed.), *The Hungarian Revolution of 1956* (1996).

The Soviets also suppressed the Hungarian Revolution for ideological reasons. During these years Soviet attempts to enlarge the world communist empire centred on the Third World. The Soviet leadership could well imagine the damage that might be done to these expansion efforts if Hungary were to be seen restoring multiparty democracy by way of an anti-Soviet uprising nearly ten years after the institution of communism.

The Soviets regarded the following elements to be of greatest importance to the maintenance of the communist system in the eastern European satellite states: a competent and unified Communist Party leadership; a powerful and resolute state security apparatus; a loyal and disciplined armed force and military leadership; and a strict party control of all media. Any hint of unrest in any of these institutions immediately set off warning bells within the Soviet decision-making mechanism; the breakdown of all four of them at once, as happened in Hungary in 1956, left the Soviets with only one option: armed intervention.

**Source D:** from identical Notes from the Government of the Union of Soviet Socialist Republics to the Governments of France, the United Kingdom and the United States of America, 18 August 1961.

1. The Soviet Government fully understands and supports the actions of the Government of the German Democratic Republic, which established effective control on the border with West Berlin in order to bar the way for the subversive activity being carried out from West Berlin against the G.D.R. and other countries of the socialist community.

In its measures on the borders the Government of the G.D.R. merely made sure the ordinary right of any sovereign state for the protection of its interests. Any state establishes on its borders with other states such rules as it deems necessary to its legitimate interests.

2. West Berlin has been transformed into a centre of subversive activity, diversion, and espionage against the G.D.R., the Soviet Union, and other socialist countries. Former and present West Berlin municipal leaders have cynically called West Berlin an "arrow in the living body of the German Democratic Republic" . . . The gates of West Berlin have been opened to international criminals of all kinds, if only to sharpen international tension and widen the provocations against the countries of the socialist community.

**Source E:** from an address by the Vice-President of the United States of America, Lyndon B. Johnson, to the Berlin Parliament, 19 August 1961.

This crisis has arisen because of a massive fact of history. The free men of Germany—both here and in West Germany—have succeeded in these years since the end of the war beyond our most optimistic hopes. I am not referring only to their economic success, which all the world knows and admires. They succeeded in far more important ways. They have built a vital democratic life. They have accepted with admirable self-discipline restraints on their military establishment. They have played a great constructive role in making a united Europe.

Meanwhile, in East Germany there has been a terrible and tragic failure. Despite every instrument of force and propaganda, despite every asset of German skill and German resources, the Communists have not been able to create a life to which men can commit their talents, their faith and the future of their children.

Make no mistake. This fact of history is well understood in the Kremlin. What they are trying to do now is to interpose barbed wire, bayonets and tanks against the forces of history.

**Source F:** from J. Sutterlin and D. Klein, *Berlin: From Symbol of Confrontation to Keystone of Stability* (1989).

Although the Western powers were expecting drastic communist action to stem the East German refugee flow, the act of building the wall took them by surprise. There were no contingency plans for such an event. The Berlin garrison was strengthened. Otherwise, the Western reaction was largely limited to spirited but totally ineffective protests.

The West took comfort in the belief that the wall reflected basic Soviet weakness rather than strength. Communism, far from being on the march, could only maintain its dominance by holding a people captive. Moreover, it was quickly perceived that the wall might increase stability in an otherwise volatile area, thereby reducing the risk of armed confrontation.

**Source G:** from the National Security Action Memorandum 288 of 17 March 1964.

We seek an independent non-Communist South Vietnam. We do not require that it serve as a Western base or as a member of a Western Alliance. South Vietnam must be free, however, to accept outside assistance as required to maintain its security. This assistance should be able to take the form not only of economic and social measures but also police and military help to root out and control insurgent elements.

Unless we can achieve this objective in South Vietnam, there are three possibilities for almost all of Southeast Asia:

- it will probably fall under Communist dominance (all of Vietnam, Laos and Cambodia), *or*
- it will accommodate to Communism so as to remove effective U.S. and anti-Communist influence (Burma), *or*
- it will fall under the domination of forces not now explicitly Communist but likely then to become so (Indonesia taking over Malaysia).

Thailand might hold out for a period without help, but would be under grave pressure. Even the Philippines would become shaky, and the threat to India on the West, Australia and New Zealand to the South, and Taiwan, Korea and Japan to the North and East would be greatly increased.

**Source H:** from G.C. Herring, *America's Longest War: The United States and Vietnam 1950–1975* (1996 edn.).

Nowhere was the impact of Vietnam greater than on American foreign policy. The war . . . left Americans confused and deeply divided on the goals to be pursued and the methods used. The traumatic experience of Vietnam took place at the same time as the apparent improvement of relations with the Soviet Union and China and a growing concentration on domestic problems. Together, these caused a drastic change in national priorities. From the late 1940s to the 1960s, foreign policy had headed the list of national concerns, but by the mid 1970s it was well down the list . . .

The Vietnam experience also provoked strong opposition to military intervention abroad, even in defence of America's oldest and staunchest allies. Polls taken shortly before the fall of Saigon indicated that only 36% of the American people felt that the United States should make and keep commitments to other nations.

[*END OF SOURCES FOR SPECIAL TOPIC 12*]

## SPECIAL TOPIC 13: IRELAND 1900–1985: A DIVIDED IDENTITY

**Study the sources below and then answer the questions in the accompanying question paper.**

**Source A:** from a speech by Padraig Pearse at a mass meeting in Dublin, 31 March 1912.

There are as many men here as would destroy the British Empire if they were united and did their utmost. We have no wish to destroy the British, we only want our freedom. There are two sections of us—one that would be content to remain under the British Government in our own land, another that never paid, and never will pay, homage to the King of England. I am of the latter, and everyone knows it. But I should think myself a traitor to my country if I did not answer the summons of this gathering, for it is clear to me that the Bill which we shall support to-day will be for the good of Ireland and that we shall be stronger with it than without it. I am not accepting the Bill in advance. We may have to refuse it. We are only here to say that the voice of Ireland must be listened to henceforward. Let us unite and win a good Act from the British; I think it can be done. But if we are tricked this time, there is a party in Ireland, and I am one of them, that will advise the Irish People to have no counsel or dealings with the British for ever again, but to answer them henceforward with the strong hand and the sword's edge. Let the British understand that if we are cheated once more there will be red war in Ireland.

**Source B:** members of the Ulster Volunteer Force, 1913.

**Source C:** from D.G. Boyce, *Ireland 1828–1923: From Ascendancy to Democracy* (1992).

The home rule crisis provided Unionism, and especially Ulster Unionism, with just that kind of atmosphere which could mould the Protestants of the north of Ireland into a single, compact community. Ulster Protestants could be represented to Britain and the world as a distinct group of people, progressive, orderly and loyal, whose only wish was to remain in the United Kingdom, not to be handed over to their traditional enemies and the enemies of the empire. They did not base their claim, as nationalists did, on some immemorial, historical right. They based it upon their constitutional and legal rights as subjects of the Crown, but they had a lively sense of the Protestant past, which they interpreted as one of heroic resistance to oppression and tyranny. They thus telescoped that past, giving it a unity and a coherence that it hardly possessed. They did not assert a nationalist identity. On the contrary, they held that nationalism was a sham, and could not be made the basis of politics at all. It would weaken the kingdom and the empire, and open the way to the decline of both.

**Source D:** from a speech in the House of Commons by David Lloyd George, 23 October 1917.

I have read the speeches of the Honourable Member for East Clare [de Valera]. They are not excited and so far as language is concerned they are not violent. They are plain, deliberate, and I might almost say cold-blooded incitements to rebellion . . . And he delivered them not merely on one occasion. He has repeated them at meeting after meeting almost in the same studied terms . . . urging the people to train, to master their rifles, to study their mechanism in order that whenever they are supplied with rifles they should be able to use them efficiently . . . That is not a case of violent, abusive, and excitable language. It is the case of a man of great ability, of considerable influence deliberately going down to the district . . . to stir people up to rebellion against the authorities.

There is a great deal of talk among the Sinn Féiners which does not mean Home Rule. It does not mean self-government. It means complete separation . . . it means secession. The words which are used are "sovereign independence". This country could not possibly accept that under any conditions.

**Source E:** from a speech by Eamon de Valera on being elected President of Sinn Féin, 25 October 1917.

The Constitution of this new movement which you have adopted is one which it may be well to lay stress on. It says that this organisation of Sinn Féin aims at securing international recognition of Ireland as an independent Irish republic. That is what I stand for, what I stood for in East Clare; and it is because I stand for that, that I was elected here. I said in East Clare when I was elected that I regarded that election as a monument to the dead. I regard my election here as a monument to the brave dead, and I believe that this is proof that they were right, that what they fought for—the complete and absolute freedom and separation from England—was the pious wish of every Irish heart.

**Source F:** from F.S.L. Lyons, *Ireland since the Famine* (1985).

All the passion, all the determination which Sinn Féin had been able to mobilise against the threat of military service was thrown behind it in the general election of 1918. It did not matter that many of the Sinn Féin candidates were still in prison, or that their manifesto was heavily censored by the authorities. On the contrary, these government attentions were an added advantage and certainly did not prevent them from getting their message home to the electorate.

What was that message? It was to be achieved by a four-point policy. These four points were: first—withdrawal from Westminster; second—"making use of any and every means available to render impotent the power of England to hold Ireland in subjection by military force"; third—the establishment of a constituent assembly as the supreme national authority; and finally—to appeal to the Peace Conference "for the establishment of Ireland as an independent nation".

Such a programme proved irresistible. The lure and glamour of the republic carried everything before it.

**Source G:** from a statement by a British Government spokesman, 1920.

They did not wait for the usual uniform, these Black and Tans who have joined the Royal Irish Constabulary. They came at once. They know what danger is. They have looked death in the eyes before and did not flinch. They will not flinch now. They will go on with the job—the job of making Ireland once again safe for the law-abiding, and an appropriate hell for those whose trade is agitation, and whose method is murder.

**Source H:** The jury verdict at an inquest in Cork, March 1920.

We find that the late Alderman MacCurtain, Lord Mayor of Cork, died from shock and haemorrhage caused by bullet wounds, and that he was wilfully murdered under circumstances of the most callous brutality, and that the murder was organised and carried out by the Royal Irish Constabulary, officially directed by the British government. We return a verdict of wilful murder against David Lloyd George, Prime Minister of England; Lord French, Lord Lieutenant of Ireland; Ian MacPherson, late Chief Secretary of Ireland; Acting Inspector General Smith, of the Royal Irish Constabulary.

[*END OF SOURCES FOR SPECIAL TOPIC 13*]

[*END OF SOURCES*]

SCOTTISH CERTIFICATE OF EDUCATION 1999

THURSDAY, 13 MAY
1.30 PM – 3.30 PM

# HISTORY
# HIGHER GRADE
## Paper II
## Questions

### SPECIAL TOPIC 1: NORMAN CONQUEST AND EXPANSION 1050–1153

**Answer *all* of the following questions.** *Marks*

1. In what ways does **Source A** cast doubt on the reliability of William of Poitiers as a chronicler of the Norman Conquest? **4**

2. Was William justified in invading England? **6**

3. To what extent does **Source B** explain the Norman victory at Hastings? **5**

4. How far does **Source C** support Golding's views about William's policies (**Source D**)? **5**

5. How useful is **Source E** in explaining William's conquest and control of England? **6**

6. To what extent did William destroy Anglo-Saxon society? Refer to **Sources C**, **D**, **E** and **F** and your own knowledge. **8**

7. Does **Source G** compare adequately the "Norman" takeovers of Scotland and England? **5**

8. Do you agree that the Norman achievement in Europe between 1050 and 1153 was only a myth created by the Norman chroniclers? **6**

**(45)**

[*END OF QUESTIONS ON SPECIAL TOPIC 1*]

1999

## SPECIAL TOPIC 2: THE CRUSADES 1096–1204

**Answer *all* of the following questions.** *Marks*

**1.** How fully does **Source A** explain the reasons for the fall of Jerusalem in 1187? 6

**2.** How reliable is **Source B** as evidence of the reasons for Philip's departure from the Third Crusade? 4

**3.** To what extent does the evidence in **Source C** support the views of Riley–Smith in **Source D**? 5

**4.** Compare the views of **Sources E** and **F** about the murder of Conrad of Montferrat. 4

**5.** In your opinion, who was responsible for Conrad's murder? Refer to **Sources E** and **F** and your own knowledge. 6

**6.** Is there sufficient evidence in **Source G** to argue that Richard was a great military leader? 6

**7.** Evaluate the views of Davis (**Source H**) on the Third Crusade by considering the evidence in **Sources B**, **E** and **G** and your own knowledge. 8

**8.** How far did the failure of the Third Crusade lead to a decline of the crusading movement in the thirteenth century? 6

**(45)**

[*END OF QUESTIONS ON SPECIAL TOPIC 2*]

## SPECIAL TOPIC 3: TRADE AND TOWNS

**Answer *all* of the following questions.**

**1.** Compare the views expressed in **Sources A** and **B** about the relationship between burghs and feudalism. 5

**2.** How fully does **Source A** explain the origins of towns in Scotland? 6

**3.** To what extent does **Source C** illustrate the hierarchical structure of Scottish burghs in the fifteenth century? 6

**4.** How valuable is **Source D** as evidence of the development of burgh government in the fifteenth century? 5

**5.** In what ways do **Sources E** and **F** differ in their views of relations between merchants and craftsmen in fifteenth-century burghs? 5

**6.** How important was rivalry between merchants and craftsmen in fifteenth-century Scottish burghs? Refer to **Sources E**, **F** and **G** and your own knowledge. 8

**7.** How reliable is **Source G** as evidence of urban unrest in Scotland in the early fifteenth century? 4

**8.** Why was there much less urban unrest in Scotland than in the rest of Europe during the fourteenth and fifteenth centuries? 6

**(45)**

[*END OF QUESTIONS ON SPECIAL TOPIC 3*]

## SPECIAL TOPIC 4: SCOTLAND 1689–1715

**Answer *all* of the following questions.** *Marks*

1. How valuable is **Source A** as evidence of the arguments of supporters of the Union? 4
2. To what extent do **Sources A** and **B** agree over the idea of a federal union? 4
3. How significant were the issues raised in **Sources B**, **C** and **D** in the debate over Scottish identity before 1707? 8
4. Why did relations between Scotland and England deteriorate between 1701 and 1705? 5
5. How important was the Squadrone Volante in passing the Act of Union? Refer to **Source E** and your own knowledge. 6
6. How fully do **Sources F** and **G** illustrate the opposition to the Union in Scotland before 1707? 6
7. How far do you accept the assessment of the Treaty of Union in **Source D**? 6
8. How typical were the opinions of Seafield, as described in **Source H**, of those held by Scots between 1707 and 1715? 6

**(45)**

*[END OF QUESTIONS ON SPECIAL TOPIC 4]*

## SPECIAL TOPIC 5: THE ATLANTIC SLAVE TRADE

**Answer *all* of the following questions.**

1. What benefits did Britain gain by becoming involved in the Slave Trade? 6
2. How valuable is **Source A** as evidence of the experience of African slaves? 4
3. How accurate a description do **Sources A** and **B** give of the treatment of slaves in the Middle Passage? 6
4. To what extent do you accept Oldfield's views (**Source C**) about the impact of the American revolution on British attitudes to the Slave Trade? 6
5. Which of the methods used by the abolitionists were most effective in promoting their cause? Refer to **Sources D**, **E**, and **F** and your own knowledge. 8
6. Compare **Sources G** and **H** as evidence of the economic importance of the Slave Trade. 5
7. How typical is **Source H** of the arguments put forward by supporters of the Slave Trade? 5
8. How great was the impact of the British abolition in 1807 on the Slave Trade as a whole? 5

**(45)**

*[END OF QUESTIONS ON SPECIAL TOPIC 5]*

## SPECIAL TOPIC 6: THE AMERICAN REVOLUTION

**Answer *all* of the following questions.** *Marks*

1. How accurate a description does **Source A** give of British control of the North American colonies? 6
2. How useful is **Source B** as evidence of feelings in Britain about the American conflict? 5
3. To what extent does the evidence in **Source D** confirm the views expressed in **Source C**? 4
4. How fully does **Source E** describe the impact of Paine's *Common Sense* on American opinion? 5
5. To what extent do **Sources A**, **C** and **E** describe the issues at stake in the conflict between Britain and the American colonies? 8
6. Why did it become impossible to resolve these issues without fighting? 6
7. How important was military leadership to the outcome of the war? Refer to **Sources F** and **G** and your own knowledge. 7
8. Comment on the historical significance of **Source H**. 4

**(45)**

[*END OF QUESTIONS ON SPECIAL TOPIC 6*]

## SPECIAL TOPIC 7: THE ENLIGHTENMENT IN SCOTLAND

**Answer *all* of the following questions.**

1. How typical was **Source A** of the attitudes of Enlightenment thinkers to contemporary politics and society? 6
2. To what extent do you accept **Source B**'s analysis of the origins of the Scottish Enlightenment? 6
3. How fully does **Source C** describe the role of the Moderate clergy in the intellectual life of later eighteenth-century Scotland? 6
4. Compare the views of Adam Smith (**Source D**) and David Hume (**Source E**) about human self interest. 4
5. How important were European influences in Scottish art and architecture during the Enlightenment? Refer to **Source F** and your own knowledge. 5
6. To what extent do **Sources C**, **D** and **F** illustrate the range of Scotland's contribution to the Enlightenment? 8
7. How useful is **Source G** as evidence of the changes in Highland society in the late eighteenth century? 5
8. How typical was the career of Archibald Grant of Monymusk (**Source H**) of agricultural improvers? 5

**(45)**

[*END OF QUESTIONS ON SPECIAL TOPIC 7*]

## SPECIAL TOPIC 8: PATTERNS OF MIGRATION: SCOTLAND 1830s–1930s

**Answer *all* of the following questions.** *Marks*

1. To what extent does the evidence in **Source A** support the views of Checkland (**Source B**)? 5

2. How valuable is **Source C** as evidence of living conditions in Victorian Scotland? 4

3. How accurately does **Source D** reflect Scottish attitudes at the time towards Irish immigrants? 5

4. How far do you accept Devine's explanation (**Source E**) for the poor living conditions of Irish immigrants in the 1830s and 1840s? 5

5. How fair is it to argue that migration caused living conditions in Scotland to deteriorate during the nineteenth century? Refer to **Sources D**, **E** and **F** and your knowledge. 8

6. How well does **Source G** illustrate the attitudes of Irish immigrants towards education? 6

7. How fully does **Source H** explain the difficulties faced by Irish immigrants in becoming part of the wider Scottish community? 6

8. Was hardship at home or opportunity abroad more important in causing emigration from Scotland between the 1830s and 1930s? 6

**(45)**

[*END OF QUESTIONS ON SPECIAL TOPIC 8*]

## SPECIAL TOPIC 9: THE THIRD FRENCH REPUBLIC 1871–1914

**Answer *all* of the following questions.**

1. How valuable is **Source A** as evidence of workers' attitudes towards the Republic? 4

2. To what extent does the evidence in **Source B** support the views of Moss (**Source C**) about the activities of French trade unions? 5

3. How fully do **Sources D** and **E** illustrate the issues that arose between Church and State under the Third Republic? 7

4. How far do you accept the assessment by Ravitch (**Source F**) of the results of the Law of Separation? 5

5. To what extent do **Sources A**, **C** and **F** reveal the divisions in French society under the Third Republic? 8

6. How serious a threat were political extremists to the survival of the Republic? 6

7. What justification is there for the views expressed by Anderson in **Source G**? 5

8. How successful was the Third Republic in rebuilding France's international prestige by 1914? 5

**(45)**

[*END OF QUESTIONS ON SPECIAL TOPIC 9*]

## SPECIAL TOPIC 10: AFRICAN SOCIETIES AND EUROPEAN IMPERIALISM 1880–1914

**Answer *all* of the following questions.** *Marks*

1. How accurately does **Source A** describe the influence of religion as a motive for European colonisation in Africa? 5

2. To what extent does the evidence in **Source B** support the views of Hargreaves (**Source C**)? 5

3. How well does **Source D** illustrate German colonial ambitions in East Africa at the time? 5

4. How far did German colonial ambitions affect relations with Britain between 1885 and 1914? 6

5. What justification was there for the views expressed in **Source F**? 6

6. How fully do **Sources C**, **E** and **F** explain British government policy towards colonial expansion in Africa? 8

7. How valuable is **Source G** as evidence about the treatment of Africans by colonial governments? 4

8. Would you agree that the long-term consequences of colonial rule on African societies proved disastrous in all respects? 6

**(45)**

[*END OF QUESTIONS ON SPECIAL TOPIC 10*]

## SPECIAL TOPIC 11: APPEASEMENT AND THE ROAD TO WAR, TO 1939

**Answer *all* of the following questions.**

1. How useful is **Source A** as evidence of British public opinion towards the re-occupation of the Rhineland? 4

2. To what extent does the evidence in **Source A** support the views of Bloch in **Source B**? 5

3. How influential were the opinions expressed in **Source C** in the development of the British policy of appeasement in the 1930s? 7

4. How convincing is **Source D**'s defence of the British government's response to the Anschluss of March 1938? 5

5. To what extent did events during the 1930s justify the views expressed by Sinclair in **Source E**? 6

6. Comment on Low's interpretation of the Czechoslovakian crisis (**Source F**). 4

7. To what extent do **Sources F** and **G** reflect British opinion at the time of the Czechoslovakian crisis? 6

8. How accurate is Bartlett's analysis (**Source H**) of Chamberlain's conduct of foreign policy in 1938? Refer to **Sources D**, **E** and **G** and your own knowledge. 8

**(45)**

[*END OF QUESTIONS ON SPECIAL TOPIC 11*]

## SPECIAL TOPIC 12: THE ORIGINS AND DEVELOPMENT OF THE COLD WAR 1945–1985

**Answer *all* of the following questions.** *Marks*

1. How valuable is **Source A** in explaining the political unrest in Hungary in 1956? 4
2. How much support was there in Hungary for the actions announced by Nagy in **Source B**? 6
3. How far do you accept Litvan's explanation (**Source C**) for Soviet intervention in Hungary? 6
4. Compare the views on the origins of the Berlin crisis of 1961 expressed in **Sources D** and **E**. 4
5. To what extent do you accept **Source F**'s assessment of the outcome of the Berlin crisis? 5
6. To what extent do **Sources C**, **D**, **E** and **F** explain the continuing tension between East and West between 1945 and 1962? 8
7. How fully does **Source G** explain the reasons for American intervention in Vietnam? 6
8. How accurately does **Source H** analyse the changing aims of American foreign policy as a result of America's experience in Vietnam? 6

**(45)**

[*END OF QUESTIONS ON SPECIAL TOPIC 12*]

## SPECIAL TOPIC 13: IRELAND 1900–1985: A DIVIDED IDENTITY

**Answer *all* of the following questions.**

1. How fully does **Source A** represent the Nationalist response to the Home Rule Bill of 1912? 6
2. How valuable is **Source B** as evidence of the strength of opposition in Ulster towards the Home Rule Bill? 4
3. To what extent do you accept Boyce's assessment (**Source C**) of Ulster Unionism in the years before 1914? 6
4. How far does de Valera's speech (**Source E**) confirm the arguments put forward by Lloyd George in **Source D**? 4
5. How fully does **Source F** explain the success of Sinn Féin in the general election of 1918? 6
6. How accurately does **Source G** describe the activities of the Black and Tans in Ireland? 5
7. To what extent do **Sources D**, **E**, **G** and **H** illustrate the growing conflict between the British government and the majority of the Irish people between 1916 and 1920? 8
8. How effectively did the Government of Ireland Act of 1920 resolve this conflict? 6

**(45)**

[*END OF QUESTIONS ON SPECIAL TOPIC 13*]

[*END OF QUESTION PAPER*]

Printed by Bell & Bain Ltd., Glasgow, Scotland.